THE SMARTEST PERSON IN THE ROOM

THE
SMARTEST
PERSON IN
THE ROOM

THE ROOT CAUSE AND NEW
SOLUTION FOR CYBERSECURITY

CHRISTIAN ESPINOSA

LIONCREST
PUBLISHING

THE SMARTEST PERSON IN THE ROOM
The Root Cause and New Solution for Cybersecurity

ISBN   978-1-5445-1622-6 *Hardcover*
      978-1-5445-1621-9 *Paperback*
      978-1-5445-1620-2 *Ebook*
      978-1-5445-1623-3 *Audiobook*

CONTENTS

DISCLAIMER

There are some fantastic cybersecurity leaders and professionals out there. I'm not stating otherwise—I'm simply highlighting typical technical personality types that are hindering our ability to win the cybersecurity war.

Also, I have included hyperlinks as references throughout the book. At the time of publishing, these links are active. However, due to the volatile, unpredictable nature of the internet, these hyperlinks may stop working at any point in the future.

INTRODUCTION

When Dick Cheney, former Vice President of the United States, found out his pacemaker was hackable, he had his doctors disable its wireless feature. He was terrified he would be assassinated via his pacemaker.[1]

It sounds like fake news, but it's not. You probably don't have pacemaker assassins following you, but right now, you are surrounded by invisible thieves who want to break in and steal from you.

They aren't trying to burglarize your house or your corporate office. They aren't lurking in the bushes or wearing ski masks. The thieves I'm talking about are virtual. That's why you can't see them.

They're called cybercriminals, and they are incessantly looking for openings on your computer or in your data center. They want to steal your information for financial gain, for terrorism,

---

1   "Cheney Reveals Fear of Pacemaker Hack," ABC News (video), accessed October 20, 2020, https://abcnews.go.com/GMA/video/ dick-cheney-60-minutes-interview-reveals-fear-pacemaker-20632056.

or something far more nefarious—and maybe some of these criminals are trying to hack into your life-dependent medical device as Dick Cheney feared.

Whatever their motivation is, it doesn't matter; cybercriminals want to steal your information to wreak havoc.

This matters because you are responsible for protecting your company's data. You may be the CEO, COO, or CISO of your organization, and you are accountable for keeping your client's data, your medical devices, and/or your company's patents or intellectual property (IP) safe. You are on the front lines of a war most of us cannot see, with cybercriminals on one side and the good guys, the ones trying to lock all of your virtual windows and doors to secure your data, on the other side.

If this were our house or corporate office, we'd be able to see the thieves trying to break in. Because this war is happening virtually, we don't think much of it until our personal computer has been compromised or our client or medical data has been stolen. Most of us don't realize these virtual crimes are happening until it's too late.

THE ROOT OF THE PROBLEM

Like thieves in the flesh, cybercriminals will always exist, and they will always try to hack into your network and steal your information. So what measures are the cybersecurity professionals like me taking to combat them? And are these methods working?

I would say they are not. In fact, I would go so far as to say these methods are *failing*. It seems as if every other day there is news of another major data breach. The cybercriminals are *winning*. Why?

We've had this problem for years. I have seen it as an information assurance (IA) analyst, penetration tester, cybersecurity engineer, trainer, and consultant. There isn't a piece of hardware or software that's going to solve it because the people are the real issue.

Cybersecurity is a support industry, and a lot of professionals in the industry tend to forget that. These professionals think that cybersecurity is an industry unto itself, but it wouldn't exist without other industries (like manufacturing, healthcare, and financial services). Cybersecurity, like IT, *supports* those other industries. Here's a great definition of cybersecurity:

> Measures taken to protect a computer or computer system (as on the internet) against unauthorized access or attack.[2]

Business leaders rely on their cybersecurity staff to protect their company data. I have held executive-level positions in cybersecurity firms and founded my own company, Alpine Security, and in my more than thirty years of experience in cybersecurity and leadership, I found these technical employees are the root of the problem. I've read the books and articles outlining overly complicated frameworks and best practices needed to win the cybersecurity war, but it's the people and their egos at the nexus of the industry's failings, not the other way around.

That tells me two things: we need to come up with something different, and when we do, people need to pay attention.

---

2 *Merriam-Webster*, s.v. "Cybersecurity," accessed October 20, 2020, https://www.merriam-webster.com/dictionary/cybersecurity.

THE SECURE METHODOLOGY

Right now, almost every business has a team of technical employees who contribute to the problems within the cybersecurity industry. Your people and their poor communication skills are the reason your data was stolen, not your lack of cutting-edge technology. Their need to be the smartest person in the room and their substandard people skills have rendered them unable to communicate clearly and work effectively with others to solve problems. That's why we're losing the cybersecurity war.

So what's the solution? How can you protect yourself?

In my experience, open communication allows us to solve problems and commit to fixing them. If we strengthen our communication skills, we can also strengthen our ability to win the cybersecurity war. However, successful open communication requires soft people skills, such as empathy, active listening, vulnerability, and trust.

Many technical people struggle with people skills because they're often, at their cores, insecure. They are uncomfortable interacting with others because they fear the ambiguity that goes along with it. They crave certainty and prefer things to be either black or white; most can't handle the shades of gray that come with human interaction and business politics rampant in large organizations.

Many technical people also struggle with curiosity. In public, they often lack curiosity. Yet, in private, it is my experience that technical people are very curious. Some would rather stay silent than be exposed for their lack of knowledge. These people care mainly about being the smartest person in the room, which inhibits their communication skills. Growth requires curiosity, but fear of judgment prevents many technical folk from communicating effectively at work and solving problems in cybersecurity.

Dealing with other people isn't nearly as ambiguous as it appears, though. There are simple, clear, and prioritized steps to develop and refine the people skills needed to enhance communication and improve interactions with others. Simple does not mean easy, though. I want to make that clear.

Introducing the Secure Methodology, a step-by-step guide designed to show you exactly how to boost your technical staff's people skills in order to have open, honest, and effective communication. When the communication within your organization is improved, you will be better equipped to win the cybersecurity war because everyone will be on the same page and working together to fight cybercrime.

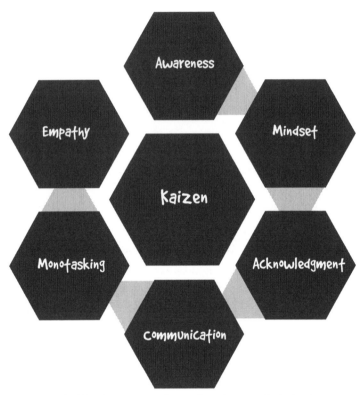

The Secure Methodology has seven steps. The seventh step, kaizen, applies both to the individual steps and the methodology as a whole.

THE SECURE METHODOLOGY OVERVIEW

- Step 1: Awareness. Awareness of ourselves and the world around us empowers us with options.
- Step 2: Mindset. Our mind is a powerful tool that we can use to our advantage or disadvantage.
- Step 3: Acknowledgment. Acknowledgment of ourselves and others reminds us of what we are capable of and motivates us.
- Step 4: Communication. Our fulfillment in life boils down to how well we communicate with ourselves and others.

- Step 5: Monotasking. Presence is our ally; distraction is our enemy.
- Step 6: Empathy. Our inner demons, successes, and failures connect us to humanity.
- Step 7: Kaizen. Continuous improvement is necessary for evolution.

This methodology isn't esoteric; its steps are tangible—meaning it will appeal to employees with a technical, black-and-white mindset. When the methodology is applied, technical employees will learn to actually listen and communicate, which will not only strengthen internal relationships, but it will boost relationships with clients as well. Within the pages of this book, I will show you how to enhance their overall awareness, change their mindsets, and increase their empathy, and you, as the company leader, will benefit because your internal communication with your cybersecurity and technical team will be more transparent, your data will be more secure, and you'll be able to trust your technical staff with your clients.

The bonus is that the lives of your technical staff will improve as well. When the tools outlined in this book are applied and maintained, your employees will be respected and admired by their managers, peers, and subordinates. They are invested in protecting the client's data from cybercriminals, and they become heroes.

This book isn't just for company executives and technical leaders; it's also for people on the front lines of the cyberwar. If you are a technical employee, currently struggling to take your career to the next level, this book is for you, too. This book will show you how you can enhance your people and life skills so you're happier, satisfied, and more fulfilled, both at work and at home.

Finally, if you simply want insight into the minds of technical employees (or the issues that, in my opinion, are plaguing the cybersecurity industry), this book is also for you. Maybe you're curious as to why your data keeps getting stolen. Or maybe you have a vested interest in a company responsible for protecting data. Maybe you're reading this book to glean insights, hoping to see something helpful that company leadership missed. If that's you, this book is for you to read, too.

MY NEED FOR CERTAINTY AND SIGNIFICANCE

I know what it's like to be a technical employee because I used to be one, and I know how to communicate with *most* of them. I don't want to give the impression that I've got it all figured out because mastery is a journey and takes time. Daily, I face situations that are still challenging for me.

For the majority of my three-decade career in cybersecurity, I wanted to be the smartest person in the room. My need for certainty and significance was so strong that I simply didn't care about anything else. I led with my ego and postured and bullied my way through meetings; my people skills were subpar.

My childhood in both California and Arkansas was unstable, uncertain, and chaotic. I craved certainty and significance and would do whatever I needed to do to have both. After I graduated high school, I was accepted into all three major military academies (Air Force, Army, and Navy) but chose the Air Force Academy in Colorado Springs because I wanted to fly jets, similar to Tom Cruise in *Top Gun*, one of my all-time favorite movies. I received my degree in engineering, took my first cybersecurity training at Keesler Air Force Base in Biloxi, Mississippi, and then my first assignment at Brooks Air Force Base in San Antonio, Texas.

In the military, I was first exposed to the aspects of cybersecurity because you have to secure your data, keep confidential documents safe, and secret networks hidden. Those were my primary responsibilities on all of my military assignments.

I was active duty for six years. During this time, I developed and built computer networks (network engineering) and installed them. My systems are still in place at the BWI (Baltimore-Washington International) and SeaTac International Airports.

After I separated from the Air Force and settled in the St. Louis, Missouri area, I started my new civilian career as a contractor for the Air Force. I joined what used to be an elite unit, ScopeNet, where I traveled from Air Force base to Air Force base across the globe to help optimize network security and efficiency.

From there, I took a contract position with the Department of Homeland Security (DHS) where I designed threat scenarios and then trained people on how to respond to them. After that, I took a VP of Security Products position with a commercial company, where I was responsible for penetration testing and cybersecurity assessments for commercial aircraft (on ground and in air).

It was at this point that my life started to change.

THE DEFINING MOMENT

Up until I became the VP for a corporate company, I had craved certainty and significance, but while I was there, all that changed. Those two needs had gotten me far in my career, but now they were *hindering* me. The things I had craved the most (for the majority of my life) were hurting both my personal and professional growth.

A TYPICAL CHILDHOOD DAY

When I was twelve, I lived in Knoxville, Arkansas, with my mom, my stepdad, and my two half brothers.

One day, I walked home from school and noticed the car (an old AMC Gremlin) wasn't in the driveway. My mom didn't work (she never did), so it was a surprise when the car was missing.

I could hear loud music coming from the house, though, so I went inside. The scene before me was nothing short of chaotic. My two younger brothers were bloody, with bandages on their heads, and my mom was sitting at the dining room table eating raw hamburger meat, straight from the package, with her fingers.

With one look, I could tell she was out of her mind on drugs and alcohol. When I asked my brothers what happened, I found out she had flipped the car, with my brothers in it. She was headed back from Scranton, Arkansas, the closest town in a wet county, with her daily booze rations. (Knoxville was in Johnson Country, Arkansas, a dry county, so she couldn't buy alcohol there.)

This was just a typical day in my childhood. There was zero certainty, which is why I craved it so much.

I realized I had sought after certainty and significance for so long that I had become too comfortable. I had a stable job and a house with a proverbial white picket fence. I was high up in my company and the best at my job, and coming from my background, that was a success.

The problem was that I wasn't happy. I had everything I thought I wanted, but I still wasn't fulfilled. I was happy by society's definition of success, but I felt as if there was a void. I didn't mind the long hours, but there was a little voice inside me telling me there was something more. I was working to climb the ladder of success and make as much money as possible, but I wasn't doing it from a place of fulfillment or alignment with who I felt I was. This incongruence was killing me inside.

So I quit. I walked into the CEO's office, without another job lined up, and gave her my notice.

That was the first time in my life where I didn't have everything all planned out. I had never quit a job without having another one to fall back on, but I didn't care. I knew I needed to change something in order to be happy and to grow personally and professionally, and I knew I would figure it out. I knew I could be resourceful.

We are all fighting an internal war started by our own egos. Our insecurities stem from thoughts like, *Am I good enough? Do I matter? What if I look stupid? What will everyone think?* We can resolve these insecurities by growing internally and dissolving the ego, but until we do, we cannot effectively fight the cybersecurity war.

That was a defining moment for me and started me down a

path that led to starting my own cybersecurity company. I had reached a critical moment where certainty and significance no longer mattered as much. For my entire life to that point, I had wanted so badly to be the best at everything, I never wanted to admit I didn't have it all figured out or that I needed help, and my connections and relationships suffered for it.

Then suddenly, for the first time in my life, I valued growth, contribution, and *un*certainty more than significance and certainty. I no longer needed to be the smartest person in the room. I wanted to get better and *be* better. I wanted to be a better person, not just a more "successful" person. I had hit the ceiling at work (and in life) and knew something needed to change in order for me to grow.

I knew this transition wouldn't be easy. I knew it would take work and reflection to identify how my insecurities were manifesting in the workplace and hindering my growth professionally.

So I started my personal journey and did a lot of deep inner work to better understand my beliefs, needs, values, behaviors, and limitations. I wanted to know myself better. I read books, completed exercises, participated in activities all geared to help me learn who I was. I attended conference after conference and event after event. I made myself extremely uncomfortable but knew I needed to in order to change.

LANDMARK FORUM

When I first started attending events, I was so uncomfortable I would purposely excuse myself to "go to the bathroom" when it was time for group activities or sharing. I would then go for a walk or pretend to be on my phone until they were over.

At one event in particular (Landmark Forum), I felt like sneaking out and never coming back. I almost left after the first break (seriously) because interacting and being vulnerable with strangers and sharing personal details wasn't natural or easy for me.

I ended up sticking it out because I knew transformation was necessary. My resistance to these group activities and sharing exercises was reflective of my resistance to change. As I changed, however, my resistance to sharing and being vulnerable weakened. Now when I'm at an event, the group activities are my favorite part.

At one of the events I attended, I learned about the Dickens Process, a neuro-linguistic programming (NLP) process that asks you to look at your entire life and identify moments that shape how you interact today. Unresolved traumas and insecurities, which often happen in childhood but can happen later, typically play out for the rest of our lives. The awareness I gained through the Dickens Process was one of the things I learned along my journey that changed my life.

The key here is continued learning and understanding. You cannot read one book or attend one event and expect everything to magically fall in place. This is a lifelong process because it's easy to fall back into old habits.

THE DICKENS PROCESS

The Dickens Process is based on the character Ebenezer Scrooge from Charles Dickens's novella, *A Christmas Carol*. In the story, Scrooge meets a ghost on Christmas morning who shows him what his future could be if he doesn't change his current bad behavior (and limiting beliefs). This causes so much pain for Scrooge that he decides to change his ways—and his life—forever.

Jeff Bezos of Amazon fame uses the Dickens Process for decision making. In an interview, he was asked why he is so successful. He told them when it comes to decisions, he thinks about his life as an eighty-year-old man. He then chooses the option that will minimize regrets.[3]

Most of us go through life not being very self-aware, and it was through this deep work and at these events that I learned more about myself and how I interacted with others—I became aware that my insecurities had inhibited my ability to communicate effectively (as well as create genuine human connections at work). I had been afraid of being called out for something I didn't know, because I hadn't been centered enough to be okay with having a lack of knowledge about anything relevant to my job or expertise. Thanks to the insights those events provided me, I was able to learn the skills needed to connect with others and communicate effectively. Today, when I don't know something, I quickly admit it because I look at it as an opportunity to learn.

When I embarked on my personal journey, I improved my people skills and my life got better; I became a better communicator, both at work and at home. I had learned the secret to success was clear, concise communication, and human connection and that my insecurities had been holding me back.

Then a light bulb went off. Was it possible the same insecurities that had hindered my personal and professional growth were also hindering the effectiveness and growth of the cybersecurity industry?

---

3   "How the Dickens Process Can Change Your Life Forever!" Tools from Books, October 10, 2017, https://www.toolsfrombooks.com/2017/10/how-the-dickens-process-can-change-your-life/.

I would say the majority of the people in technical, cybersecurity roles are a lot like the old me. They crave significance and certainty, and posture and bully at work (and at home) to hide their insecurities. For the most part, their people skills are virtually nonexistent, which negatively impacts their ability to communicate and be effective.

Could the key to winning the cybersecurity war be as simple as increasing awareness and improving the people skills of the industry's technical staff?

ARE YOU LOOKING FOR A SILVER BULLET?

Many people are looking for a "silver bullet," a new technology or piece of hardware that will solve all of their problems. We see this all the time in the industry with next-generation firewalls, artificial intelligence (AI)-based security devices, secure clouds, and more. Yet, data breaches continue daily.

This book is not about a silver bullet. There is no overnight solution that will activate your employees' people skills or win the cybersecurity war, but I can attest that improved people skills *do* lead to better cybersecurity.

The Smartest Person in the Room will help teach you and your technical staff the people skills, life skills, and basic methodology needed to succeed in your jobs and beat cybercriminals. This book will help you and your team identify underlying issues and insecurities that keep them from thriving in the workplace, at home, and in day-to-day life. Again, if your technical staff isn't thriving in the workplace, your data is at risk.

This book is focused on helping you, a company executive,

quash your technical employees' insecurities, so they can communicate more effectively and better protect your company data, medical device, or IP. The steps outlined in this book can be applied to help technical people of all skill levels and roles and isn't geared toward a particular gender or race. I believe in the *human* race, and the issues and problems this book will help solve can be seen everywhere and in all walks of life.

We are all fighting an internal war driven by ego and our desire to be significant. This war programs and powers our insecurities, so it's important to focus on similarities, not differences. When we focus on similarities, we feel more connected and more secure within ourselves. We have less of an ego. Because we are all fighting this internal war, the lessons in this book can be applied to all humans everywhere.

The issues and problems outlined in this book don't solely revolve around the cybersecurity industry either. The contents within are geared toward executives and their technical employees, but the same insecurities, posturing, and egotism I've seen damage the cybersecurity industry can damage other industries as well.

I've also seen these detrimental traits harm personal relationships with friends, family, and loved ones.

This is a book about people skills and life skills, but it isn't a book about resolving past traumas or psychology. I *am* certified as an NLP practitioner, Time Line Therapy practitioner, and a Certified High Performance Coach (CHPC), and I *will* explore some of those theories and practices within the contents of this book, but that's about as far as I will go. I'm a proponent of NLP presuppositions (beliefs); where relevant, these will be discussed at a very high level throughout this book. If you're looking for a book promising to do a therapeutic deep dive, you should put this book down immediately and revisit Amazon.com.

Last but certainly not least, this also isn't a book about me. I will use my personal experiences to help illustrate specific points, but this is a book about you. My stories and references to my background are meant to support my arguments, nothing more. Ego is the biggest issue impacting how technical (and nontechnical) people interact with others, so I will do my best to leave mine at the door.

A SIMPLE REQUEST

I'm going to walk you through the steps of the Secure Methodology, but before I do, I'd like to make a request of you. Throughout this book, you will find activities to help you and your technical staff develop the people skills needed to win the cybersecurity war. I'd like you to take the time to think through them and complete them.

Reading about something is different than actually doing it. (I refer to people like this as paper tigers—more on them later.) Typically, you remember what you do, so for most people, the action is what reinforces the idea; it's the moment that everything clicks. Taking the time to complete the activities also verifies what you're reading. It bridges the gap between theory and reality. Reflection is also important. To fully understand something, it must be studied, reflected on, and practiced. Constant reflection is key.

I told you earlier that the Secure Methodology is tangible, and I wasn't kidding. This book is about taking action, and completing the activities inside this book will help your technical team improve their people skills. And when they do, they will be better equipped to fight cybercriminals and win the cybersecurity war. (They'll be able to fight and win their own internal war, too.)

We are losing the cybersecurity war. It's irrefutable. Every other day, news of a different data breach impacting the lives of millions of people hits the airwaves. Just ask Dick Cheney about his pacemaker, and he'll agree.

The debate is open as to the reasons *why* we're losing. I'll dive into that next.

CHAPTER 0

※ ※ ※

WHY ARE WE LOSING THE CYBERSECURITY WAR?

Knowing is not enough, we must apply. Willing is not enough, we must do.

—BRUCE LEE

Did you know you have to complete 1,500 hours of training to be certified to cut hair in the state of Arkansas? (I grew up from ages 12 to 18 in Clarksville, Arkansas, so I tend to use it as a point of reference.) That's roughly 37.5 weeks of dedicated training before you're let loose on the general public. If you want to cut hair in Arkansas, you've got to be passionate about it.

Cybersecurity experts on the other hand, the people who protect all your sensitive information (medical records, credit card information, Social Security number, etc.), can pass a test tomorrow and get hired the day after. No regulations mean no proper training is required. Score 70 percent or higher on a fifty-question cybersecurity quiz and you'll receive your certification. You're free to start work the same day, as many employers are eager to hire certified personnel.

Doesn't this seem a bit backward?

Don't get me wrong, I never want to get a bad haircut, but if something were to go awry, if my stylist were to accidentally give me a buzz cut or a mullet, that would be a lot easier to deal with than someone stealing my Social Security number or medical records. The fact that it's significantly easier to get certified to protect my sensitive data than it is to cut my hair underlies the problems we've seen in recent years in cybersecurity. Let's explore the causes.

CYBERSECURITY CERTIFICATIONS—PAPER TIGERS

Many people in cybersecurity think we are losing the cybersecurity war because of a lack of *certified* talent. They think we don't have people smart enough to combat these cybercriminals and that we as an industry need to pay more to attract the top talent away from our competitors. They think that's the only way we're going to win. They believe people are the problem, because they believe there aren't *enough* who are qualified. They're referring to the *quantity* of qualified candidates.

It's the *quality* of the candidates that's the problem, though. The current certification process itself has led to a shortage of qualified talent. Unlike Arkansas's beauty industry, many cybersecurity certifications are especially easy to earn. Being "certified" in cybersecurity has become something of a joke among industry leaders because anyone with an internet connection can search the web for the fifty-question, multiple-choice test and memorize the answers. Once they pass, they can quite easily get hired as an analyst or get a job protecting your data.

However, as soon as the job really gets intense, they prove they don't have the skills needed to safeguard against cybercriminals. I can't tell you how many times I have hired someone who looks really great on paper—has all the industry accreditations and certifications—but then looks like a deer in headlights when faced with a real problem. I call these types of cybersecurity professionals "paper tigers"—all growl and no teeth—and I try to avoid hiring them at all costs. The bar is dangerously low for cybersecurity certifications and often puts emphasis on skills that don't really matter. Plus, the tests are typically based on theory rather than application. You often need to temporarily suspend your view of reality and drink the cybersecurity Kool-Aid before taking certain certification exams.

PRACTICAL CERTIFICATIONS

I want to be clear—the concept of certifications is great, and there are many certifying organizations (such as CompTIA and EC-Council) that are doing the right thing. Instead of multiple-choice exams, they're moving to methods that test the practical application of cybersecurity processes. When you're being hacked in real life, no one presents you with a multiple-choice question and four options. Functional, practical certifications are fantastic and do a better job of preparing technical employees for cybersecurity in the real world.

And the problem perpetuates itself. You hire unqualified people; then, when the people who have passed these certifications get promoted into management positions and have hiring responsibilities, they tend to hire people who have passed the same certifications. They don't want to hire someone they think might be smarter than them—remember, they want to be the smartest person in the room. If they hire someone who has real-life experience, rather than a certification, their own lack of knowledge and skills may be exposed. The so-called talent shortage exists because our technical hiring managers aren't hiring qualified candidates.

I used to work with a really smart guy named Doug, and I noticed he tended to hire only people who were not an intellectual threat to him. As a result, his team continued to downgrade with each new hire, and consequently, his results suffered.

When I hired a CTO over Doug, it was the beginning of the end. Doug's insecurities took over because he saw the CTO as a threat. We were in business to help people secure highly sensitive data, but Doug was more concerned about someone in the company knowing more about cybersecurity than he did. However, Doug couldn't take it, and he didn't last long at the company after that.

You can cheat and cut corners to get a cybersecurity certification. *Most* certifications don't equate to quality talent. There are exceptions, and some certifications really do help qualify cybersecurity professionals. The majority, however, don't.

I have more than twenty-five certifications. Given my experience with them, I know firsthand that most don't single out quality talent like they claim to. Some certifications are great, but they simply aren't the panacea everyone is after. Hiring someone with a bunch of certifications doesn't mean you're hiring someone who is actually qualified to secure your data.

The alternative to certifications isn't much better, however.

FOUR-YEAR COLLEGE DEGREES

If you're thinking we can easily solve this problem and hire quality talent by requiring four-year degrees, forget it. We've tried that, and in my opinion, requiring a college education is the other reason why we're in this talent shortage predicament in the first place.

By requiring a four-year degree to work in cybersecurity, the qualified candidate pool instantly shrinks. There will naturally be less talent to choose from. Moreover, the four-year college model (like the current certifications model) has its own *foundational* challenges. The field changes faster than textbooks (and lesson plans) can be updated; how can we expect professors to keep up with the cybercriminals at that pace? Plus, there simply aren't enough qualified cybersecurity university professors with real-world experience. Most understand only theory, so that's what they teach. It doesn't matter if theory is different than reality.

There are two distinct categories of universities. **Traditional universities** are research-driven, and this extends to their teaching methods. **Universities of applied sciences** on the other hand are more practice-oriented with the goal of educating students for professional work life. Universities of applied sciences are a little bit better than traditional universities (and their degrees more relevant to cybersecurity) but not by much. Neither adequately prepares its students for a real-life career in cybersecurity.

For two years, I was a cybersecurity professor at a university of applied sciences in St. Louis and taught a master's-level ethical hacking class, but instead of creating lesson plans and using textbooks similar to those my colleagues were using, my lesson plans were based on real scenarios. At first, I was excited about my new gig, but it quickly soured when nearly half the students began complaining about their assignments.

They said the class was too hard for them.

Here I was, trying to teach my students advanced cybersecurity techniques, but it was clear they didn't want to work hard to learn the skills they needed to succeed in the industry. (What would someone with nearly thirty years of experience working in the field know anyway?) They wanted the *academic* cybersecurity degree, but they weren't passionate about cybersecurity in *practice*—or their ideas about cybersecurity were far removed from the reality I know. If they had been passionate, they would have dug their heels in to figure out the assignments and pass the class. In person, I have trained more than ten thousand students in cybersecurity and leadership, and it seemed to me that the majority of this group was only in it for the money a career in cybersecurity would bring them.

So I took a step back to evaluate the system as a whole. It wasn't just the students or this university in particular; it was all universities peddling the same business model—get enough people through the program and entice employers by telling them the graduates have the skills they need to succeed in the workplace. Universities are corporations with huge marketing budgets, and in the wave of self-education, their survival is at risk. You can virtually learn anything on the internet for free now, so for many degrees and programs, universities are teetering on the verge of obsolescence.

Colleges and universities typically can't keep up with real-time cybersecurity because academic cybersecurity is very different than reality. As a result, these graduates can't possibly be ready for cybersecurity in the real world.

THE CYBERSECURITY SKILLS GAP

Many cybersecurity leaders complain about a skills gap in the industry. The certification system was created to help close the gap, but many of these leaders ignore the benefits of the newer skills-based and practical certifications. Many of these leaders received four-year college degrees and believe anyone working under them should have the same credentials. They believe if they hire someone without a degree, they are devaluing their own. (This is ego.)

Not all four-year degrees are bad—I have one—but not all are relevant to the skills needed to win the cybersecurity war. Sometimes the best candidates don't have degrees, and we shouldn't overlook them because they don't have a fancy piece of paper from a university.

As employers, we also need to take it upon ourselves to train our people. We can't rely on certifying bodies and universities to do it.

A LACK OF QUALITY TALENT

To recap so far, one of the reasons we are losing the cybersecurity war is a lack of quality talent. Applying simple solutions, such as easy-to-come-by certifications, to a complex problem doesn't fix it. The certification system doesn't work because candidates can easily look up the correct answers online and memorize them, ergo it isn't a true indication of a candidate's talent or skill in cybersecurity.

Most four-year colleges don't work either because they can't keep up. By the time a new textbook is published (or even a new lesson plan is written), the cybersecurity industry has changed again. Four-year degrees are dated and thus aren't an indication of talent or skill either.

Personality and personnel issues contribute to the problem (remember my colleague Doug); insecurity, fear, and posturing run rampant in the cybersecurity field. And a general lack of risk comprehension and passion further complicate the solution.

INSECURITY

Most technical people need to be the smartest person in the room, but this need stems from insecurity rather than confidence.

A myriad of possible reasons exist for their insecurity, but I think many technical people are insecure because they either know they are unqualified to do their jobs, or they worry about not the being smartest person in the room. They either graduated with a four-year degree that taught them outdated models and best practices, or they passed the certification test because they may have memorized the answers. The talent is there, but most of us aren't looking in the right place. The focus is on certifications and degrees, when it should be on cultural fit, confidence, passion, aptitude, attitude, and people skills.

Our technical people are often so insecure that they create over-complicated solutions to cybersecurity problems only they can understand. (If no one else knows what they're talking about, how will anyone know if they're wrong?)

For example, every expert under the sun has a cybersecurity best practice or framework we're supposed to use to combat cybercriminals—there are about seven thousand now—and they are all way too complicated. Most of them have checklists with hundreds of activities on them. The whole thing is overwhelming, hard to do well, and unnecessary. It's far more critical to give attention to the five most important items on that checklist, prioritized by risk, and excel at them.

This has become such a massive problem in the industry that overly complicated solutions have now become *expected* by the clients. I always recommend very simple things, and my clients often ask, "Is that it?"

If you're going to run a marathon, you begin by running half a mile. Likewise, securing a data network or medical device should be simple, at least to start.

FEAR

Because these technical people are insecure, they're also afraid to ask questions. They're afraid if they get a question in return, they won't know the answers. Often, not only are they afraid to ask questions, but they also don't know how to ask them, leaving them incapable of seeing things from their clients' perspectives.

Four-year degrees and certifications promote a formulaic approach to cybersecurity that demonstrates a lack of perspective, people skills, and critical thinking. To be successful, each solution should be tailored to each company because each company is going to have different risks.

Winning the cybersecurity war means focusing on the client's specific needs. When you're too afraid or don't know how to ask questions, it's very difficult to figure out the exact problem the client is trying to solve or the biggest risk they are facing. This results in ineffective solutions that are generalized rather than specific to the organizations they're trying to help protect.

They apply blanket recommendations no matter the environment they're commissioned to protect—the same solutions are applied to networks used by law firms, hospitals, and public schools, even though the data each organization wants to secure and the risks they face are completely different. A law firm may need to protect case data so that evidence isn't contaminated, so their cybersecurity requirements will be different than a public school that's trying to protect the information of their students.

Most people try to protect everything equally, but the reality is, if the client has critical data and systems, the priority should be to protect the critical systems first. Technical people, who are suppressed by their own egos, are too afraid to admit they don't know how to fix one thing or prioritize another. (They're also too afraid to admit they don't understand risk, but more on that in a moment.)

DEFENSIVENESS

Fear drives defensiveness, causing people to listen for agreement rather than insight. When people have such a strong desire to be right, they listen for things they can either agree or disagree with. They don't listen to learn. These technical employees are afraid of being challenged mentally, so they work day and night to maintain their intellectual status.

I used to work with a guy named Bruce who was always paranoid someone was going to ask him a question he wouldn't be able to answer. One time in particular, he was anxious about a call we had scheduled with a manufacturing prospect. They needed us to do a penetration test on one of their medical devices.

"What if their software developer asks me about something and I don't have the answer?" Bruce said, his eyes wide with fear.

I shrugged. "Why do you need the answer? You're not the application's software developer."

Bruce wasn't hearing me. He probably spent several days worrying and fretting about that call, researching everything he could about their application and the language used to write it.

And what's interesting was the software developer never asked a single question! Bruce got all worked up and bent out of shape for nothing. He cared so much about being the smartest person in the room (and didn't want to look stupid) that in order to prove it, he thought he needed to be ready to answer every question the prospect asked. Talk about stress!

What Bruce didn't understand (and probably still doesn't) was that you can't possibly prepare for every question that may be asked because you aren't the person asking! You don't know what they're thinking and you're not in their environment. You can't control their thought process.

Technical people thrive in black-and-white environments, but in truth, the world—and our interaction with it—is colored with shades of gray. That's why meetings were always so stressful for this guy. Bruce wanted to control the environment, but he couldn't because no one can. It's impossible.

POSTURING

Posturing exacerbates the problem. Bruce cared so much about looking smart that he ignored his other responsibilities in order to research the answer to every question possible. Typically, these technical people are insecure, so they posture. They pretend they know what they're doing, and they often try to "fake it till they make it."

When an employee postures, it just means they would rather hide behind a big, complicated framework or talk over someone's head than get to the root of the problem. When these technical employees don't really know what they're doing, they try to impress their clients with one- hundred-task checklists because overcomplicating the process means there is less risk of exposure for the cybersecurity professional making the recommendation. They can hide behind a big complicated list.

TOP 5 CIS CONTROLS

In cybersecurity, there are five controls that stop 85 percent of all attacks.[4]

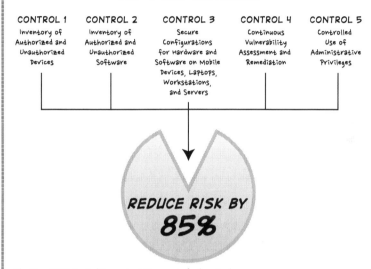

TOP 5 CIS CONTROLS

CONTROL 1	CONTROL 2	CONTROL 3	CONTROL 4	CONTROL 5
Inventory of Authorized and Unauthorized Devices	Inventory of Authorized and Unauthorized Software	Secure Configurations for Hardware and Software on Mobile Devices, Laptops, Workstations, and Servers	Continuous Vulnerability Assessment and Remediation	Controlled Use of Administrative Privileges

REDUCE RISK BY 85%

The "Top 5 CIS Controls" can stop 85 percent of cyberattacks.

If these five controls stop 85 percent of attacks, does it make sense to spend time on anything else until you've mastered them? Until these five controls are in place, does it make sense to focus on anything else?

One-hundred-item frameworks overcomplicate simple solutions, and often these five crucial controls are glossed over or ignored.

When a technical person postures, it also means they lack the confidence to ask their clients questions. This prevents them from coming up with a personalized and tailored recommenda-

---

4   "The 20 CIS Controls & Resources," Center for Internet Security, accessed October 20, 2020, https://www.cisecurity.org/controls/cis-controls-list/.

tion or solution that aligns with their clients' goals. Quite often, the questions can be the same for each client:

- *What is it you do?*
- *What are you trying to protect?*
- *What's important to your business?*

The client's responses drive the specific, customized solutions and deeper questions.

Most technical people are too afraid to ask questions, so they don't really understand the risk they're trying to safeguard against. They pretend they understand by posturing and recommending convoluted checklists, but ultimately it's too difficult for them to ask questions and tailor their solutions to meet their clients' requirements. A personalized solution means understanding risk and having the confidence to ask questions. And you can't do that if you posture.

POOR COMMUNICATION

Technical employees' unique communication style also tends to create problems in the workplace. These types of employees often use obtuse language and words and phrases like *pivoting*, *meterpreter*, CVE, SSD, and *a slash 24 subnet*, which no one else understands. There is so much technical jargon in cybersecurity that you can make a whole sentence with no real substance, and the nontechnical employees would have no idea!

Technical people love to use this jargon to talk over other people's heads (an example of this is leetspeak, which I'll tell you all about in the communication step), but more often than not, *they* don't even understand the jargon they're using.

We touched on this already, but because they're poor listeners, they're poor communicators. Instead of listening to work together to solve a problem, these types of employees listen for things to disagree with. Instead of listening to learn and better understand risk, they listen for something inaccurate so they can destroy the speaker's credibility and maintain their status as the smartest person in the room.

These communication barriers prevent open, productive communication within your company, which inhibits your team's ability to solve problems. It's no wonder that while your technical people are posturing to be the smartest person in the room, the cybercriminals are stealing your data.

RISK COMPREHENSION

I keep talking about understanding risk. All this insecurity, fear, and posturing could boil down to one thing—many technical people don't fully understand risk. With cybersecurity (and life, in general), everything boils down to risk, and the primary risk driver is the *impact* associated with the risk. If you recommend solutions to a client without understanding the real risk (the impact) or the risks from their perspective, your solutions will be useless.

In academia and on most certifications, risk is defined like this:

Risk = Threat x Vulnerability

This is a very confusing formula.

How can you define a threat or a vulnerability? How can you make this formula work in real life?

A better formula is this:

Risk = Probability x Impact

How likely is something going to happen (probability) and what's the consequence (impact) if it does?

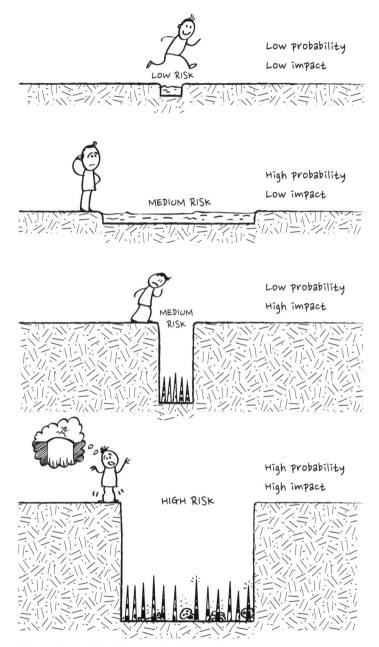

This picture best simplifies risk in terms of probability and impact.

Risk comprehension is the basic skill in cybersecurity. Cybersecurity professionals mitigate risk and secure data—it's the sole purpose of our function. Yet, many technical people in cybersecurity lack this foundational skill.

Maybe it wasn't a question on their certification exam or a required course at their college. Whatever the reason, this lack of risk comprehension complicates the industry. When you truly understand something, the solution should be simple and specific, right?

These traits work together (unfortunately) to create a vicious, downward spiral. These employees are insecure and afraid because they don't understand risk. So they posture, which only prevents them from understanding risk even more. That then leads to more insecurity, fear, and posturing. It's a never-ending cyclone of bad cybersecurity behavior.

The cybersecurity industry has a tendency to overly complicate the process because we don't understand it. So they create generalized, one-hundred-item checklists, which makes it even more difficult to identify what to protect.

If you don't understand risk, how can you know what to protect? And without knowing what to protect, how can you do great work?

PASSION

Coming up with tailored, personalized solutions (that are also simple) for every client isn't easy. It requires hard work driven by passion.

Many people get into cybersecurity as a career field because they want to make a lot of money. They could care less about data security and stopping cybercrime; they're only in it for the cash. For too many of the good guys, it's just a job.

On the other hand, cybercriminals are very passionate about stealing from you. It's their trade, their profession, and lifeblood. The risks involved with getting caught make them care strongly that they don't. Going to prison is a lot more consequential than getting written up or even losing your job.

No doubt the bad guys are passionate, and we're losing the cybersecurity war to them because most of the good guys aren't.

We've created this situation. We insist that only talent with specific degrees and/or certifications be considered, and thus, we've created a talent shortage. (Not to mention, these candidates with the degrees and certifications aren't necessarily high quality.) This talent shortage has led to aggressively overinflated salaries that attract people who come to the field only for the money. These people don't care about cybersecurity and they aren't passionate about fighting cybercrime, which means they aren't going to work very hard.

Cybercriminals, on the other hand, work day and night to figure out how to steal your information. It's clear who's in the better position to win the war.

UNPREPARED FOR REAL-LIFE CYBERCRIMINALS

Many technical employees are insecure, afraid, and posture. They have a strong desire to not only be right but also be the smartest person in the room. These "experts" don't understand risk or perspective and lack passion, so they are unable to communicate effectively with their clients and create specific solutions to their clients' problems.

They also are underqualified. Many technical people get outdated, four-year college degrees or earn cybersecurity certificates they can cheat their way through. Either path often leaves them completely unprepared for real-life cybercrime. They have no idea what they're up against.

Company leadership needs to take responsibility as well. There's too much reliance on universities and certification bodies to educate and qualify the workforce. The theory is great—degrees and certs create a pipeline of cybersecurity professionals with the knowledge, skills, and abilities to fight cybercrime. The reality differs, though. I can't reiterate this enough—we as employers must take responsibility for training our own people as well.

It's important to note not everyone wants to change—not every technical person will want to learn the people skills needed to succeed. Many will resist the lessons in this book because they have attached parts of their identity to the bad habits the Secure Methodology is designed to break. In order to change, they must first allow their identity to change, which is too much for a lot of people to handle.

SISYPHUS

I used to think everyone wanted to grow and improve in life. I spent time and money trying to help people who ultimately had no desire to grow (they lacked a growth mindset). It made me feel a lot like Sisyphus, the guy from Greek mythology whom Zeus punished and forced to push a rock up a hill, only to watch it fall back down.[5] I kept trying to pull, push, and convince them to change their mindset, yet every time they were close to a breakthrough, they would roll to the bottom of the hill again, just like that rock. Then, thinking I was the problem, I'd start the process over again.

I'm a big proponent of ownership, so I blamed myself, but as I matured, I realized people who don't want to change won't. I also realized there are a lot of people out there who do claim they want to change but still won't.

This is where their motivation—their reason why—comes into play. Without a strong reason why, it's difficult to change and move from a place of pain to a place of pleasure, the world's only two true motivators.

If we can find, train, and retain the right talent, we can end this vicious, ineffective spiral. With the right people and the right skills, we can win the cybersecurity war.

Next up: how to find the right people or teach the ones you have.

---

5   Wikipedia, s.v. "Sisyphus," last modified October 29, 2020, https://en.wikipedia.org/wiki/Sisyphus.

CHAPTER 1

WHO IS PROTECTING YOUR DATA?

The problem with cyber weapons for a country like ours is the ability to control them.

—MICHAEL HAYDEN

Are you a Star Wars fan? If you aren't, surely you've heard of it?

For those of you who haven't heard of Star Wars, it is a Disney-owned, science fiction franchise set in space that has been growing in popularity since Steven Spielberg and George Lucas released the original three films in the 1970s and 1980s.

My COO is a huge fan of the franchise. (Some would say she's obsessed with it.) She's converting her garage into an android-building workshop so she can build her own BB-8 (a popular droid Star Wars introduced in 2015) and other droids.

She's also a costume enthusiast and member of the 501st Legion, an all-volunteer organization that promotes the Star Wars brand by wearing quality costumes at public events. She plays Captain Phasma, a villain who was introduced to the franchise in 2015. She has the full outfit and headgear with interior cooling fans—apparently, it gets hot under the helmet and the fans keep the visor from fogging up and her from passing out from heat exhaustion. Legion "troop" members travel around the world for official Star Wars-related events and contribute to the community through volunteer work.

Recently, she did an event at a baseball game, but because Captain Phasma wasn't in the Star Wars movie released in 2019, she had to change her costume to make it look like she'd been struck by a light saber. So she created a long slash down the front of her suit and attached a dry-ice machine to it; the "wound" was smoking. It was one of the most inventive things I'd ever seen.

It goes without saying, my COO is quirky, and she is great at her job.

I didn't recruit her from another company or find her at a job fair—or a Star Wars event. She started out at my company as an unpaid intern because she didn't have the technical skills for a full-time gig.

She had a passion for the industry, though (much like her passion for Star Wars), and a willingness to learn and grow. She worked hard to learn the technical skills she needed to advance her career, but she also worked to develop nontechnical skills she lacked. Through that work, she deepened her people skills, learned how to communicate more effectively, and gained perspective that enhanced her problem-solving capabilities and catapulted her to the top of my organization. In a couple of years, the plan is to have her step into my shoes as the CEO. She is an incredible employee and the right person to take over the reins and continue the good fight against cybersecurity criminals. I'm constantly on the lookout for people like my COO because I want to know the best people available when I have a hiring need.

For many leaders, finding the right talent has always been a challenge. Many of us spend hundreds to thousands of dollars on executive recruiters to find them. Finding quality technical talent to entrust with your data may be even more difficult than finding a great COO, and it's something that keeps a lot of CEOs up at night.

Maybe you're one of those sleepless CEOs.

WHOM DO YOU TRUST?

As a company leader in today's digital world, your data is your biggest asset, the gold you want to protect like you're Fort Knox. Whom do you trust to secure your company data? Whom do you trust to manage your clients' data? Are you relying on a cybersecurity "expert" to keep your data safe?

If you answered yes, let me ask you a few more questions: How much do you trust this person? Do you feel confident in their abilities to secure your data? Do you sleep well at night?

Many of you don't. Many of you are worried, constantly, about the state of your data. You're worried there will be a breach and your clients' data will be stolen. Your CISO (Chief Information Security Officer) was promoted from within because they had the four-year degree and certifications in cybersecurity, but then you discovered they posture, bully, and talk over other people's heads. You may not even be aware of this because they kiss up to you and kick down those who work for them. They fail to communicate because they fail to listen. They believe they are the smartest person in the room, and as a result you have no idea what they're talking about or what they're doing. You need technical people to protect company data but are held hostage to their overcomplicated language, solutions, and checklists. It's hard to have confidence in these employees when many of them are only in it for the money and lack the people skills needed to communicate effectively. Not to mention, most of them are technically underqualified. No wonder you have a hard time sleeping at night—you don't trust your cybersecurity leadership!

SHOULD A CISO BE TECHNICAL?

A CISO is a C-level position that is often promoted from within an organization. This is often problematic because a CISO isn't a technical role. According to *Forbes*, a great CISO should have the following:

1. Communication and presentation skills
2. Policy development and administration
3. Political skills
4. Knowledge and understanding of the business and its mission
5. Collaboration and conflict management
6. Planning and strategic management
7. Supervisory skills
8. Incident management
9. Knowledge of regulations, standards, and compliance
10. Risk assessment and management[6]

---

6   Darren Death, "10 Critical Skills for a Successful CISO," *Forbes*, accessed November 13, 2020, https://councils.forbes.com/blog/ten-critical-skills-for-a-successful-ciso.

There is a very popular idea that in order to be the best at cybersecurity, you must be technical, but that isn't true. I would argue that anyone with the ten attributes listed will likely excel in a CISO role. If they have the technical skills, too, even better!

IS COMPLIANCE THE ANSWER?

A lot of company leaders put all their trust into compliance, and it impacts their hiring decisions.

The idea is, if you're compliant, you're more secure. This is not (and has never been) true, yet the idea is clung to fanatically by many company executives and even some cybersecurity leaders. So a lot of time and money is spent on compliance frameworks. Compliance frameworks help but aren't a universal solution—you can't simply follow an expensive compliance framework and expect to have an iron-clad defense. Target was certified PCI compliant two weeks before their breach. So was Heartland Payment systems.[7]

This inaccurate "compliance-equals-secure" belief is so strong that it bleeds into the hiring ideologies of many company leaders and senior cybersecurity professionals. They believe they need to "comply" with industry standards and hire only people who either have a four-year degree and/or a specific set of certifications. This practice is problematic because you end up with paper tigers!

When it comes to compliance, I often reference this diagram:

---

7   Christian Moldes, "Compliant but Not Secure: Why PCI-Certified Companies Are Being
    Breaches," *Journal of Cyber Security and Information Systems* 6, no. 1 (2018), https://www.
    csiac.org/journal-article/compliant-but-not-secure-why-pci-certified-companies-are-being-
    breached/#:~:text=In%202013%2C%20Target%20was%20certified,compliant%20for%20
    six%20consecutive%20years.

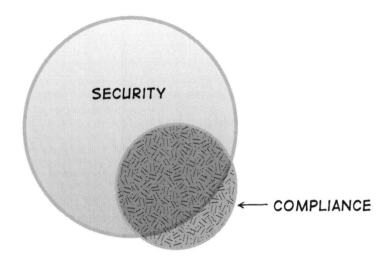

Compliance is merely a subset of security. You can't trust compliance to take care of everything, just like you can't expect that by complying with industry hiring standards, you're going to end up with a staff that's well equipped to protect your data. You have to hire *beyond* compliance. It's important, but putting all your cybersecurity eggs into the compliance basket won't solve your problems.

ALWAYS ON THE LOOKOUT

When I lived in San Antonio, I used to shop at a grocery store called HEB in the suburb of Alamo Heights. When I checked out, seven times out of ten, the same man was there to bag my groceries. He was always extremely polite, a pleasure to speak with, and he did a great job bagging. Plus, he always worked well with the cashier. Every time I saw him, his attitude was pleasant and friendly, and when I think of hiring good people, I still think of him...and that was over twenty-five years ago. Because of him, I'm always on the lookout for good people, no matter where they currently work.

HOW TO SCREEN FOR QUALIFIED TALENT

As the company leader, it is your responsibility to keep your company data and your clients' data safe. You rely heavily on the skills of your technical staff to secure you company's commodities because one mistake, one data breach, could ruin your career, your company's reputation, and the lives of everyone whose information was stolen. You are steering the ship, and the last thing you want is to go down with it because you hired the wrong person to protect your data.

Finding the right people is hard, though. There is a talent pool shortage and a cybersecurity skills gap. What are you going to do?

SCREEN FOR PEOPLE SKILLS

To find talent in a field with a massive (quality, qualified) talent shortage, we have to change our screening process. I would rather have one person who is passionate about the industry, with highly developed people skills, and a strong desire to learn than a dozen paper tigers. I don't care about four-year degrees or cybersecurity certificates. I want to work with someone who is excited about going after the bad guys; I could care less about a recent college graduate who is just in it for the money. And my recruiting benchmarks are a bit different because of it.

I look at a candidate's people skills. I look at their attitude before I look at their aptitude. If they don't pass a basic people skills test, they don't continue in the interview process.

SLOW TO HIRE AND QUICK TO FIRE

Not too long ago, I updated the hiring process at our company,

Alpine Security. We now use a TriMetrix HD[8] assessment for each candidate who passes an initial twenty-minute interview. We are slow to hire and quick to fire. The TriMetrix HD is a powerful assessment tool that combines four sciences to you to explore four key areas of performance:

1. **HOW** we behave and communicate—using the world-famous DISC assessment
2. **WHY** we move into action—using the simple yet powerful Workplace Motivators® assessment
3. **WHAT** personal talents we have at our disposal—using the TTI Acumen Capacity Index
4. **WHICH** competencies we have mastered and to what degree—using the TTI DNA® assessment

None of the skills covered in the assessment are technical. Most people make the mistake of hiring for only technical skills. Those skills are important, too, but people skills are what we should focus on.

I DIDN'T TRUST MYSELF

Several years ago, we bid on a long-term contract with a large medical device company that wanted assessment and penetration testing services. To win the bid, there were several steps to follow including an interview to see whether we were a good fit. I was tied up, so I sent good old Doug. (At the time, he was one of my best technical employees.)

Not long after the interview concluded, I received a call from a colleague who was in the interview room with Doug. Apparently, when he was asked to elaborate on something technical, he got defensive.

---

8   "TriMetrix HD," TTI Success Insights, accessed November 13, 2020, https://www.ttisuccessinsights.com.au/profiling-tools/trimetrix-hd.

He said the f-word multiple times and acted like a complete a-hole. He acted this way because his intellect was threatened and his ego bruised.

This client was very valuable to our company, so to salvage the relationship and continue to bid on the project, I called numerous people to apologize and ask for a second chance. They agreed, as long as I completed the interview myself. They also asked that Doug never be permitted to work on the project—they didn't want anything to do with him. We ended up getting the job but only because I agreed to work on the project myself.

I should have fired Doug immediately, but I didn't. I overthought it, ignored all the warning signs, and instead kept him on as an employee until he messed up a few more times, couldn't handle the heat, and quit on his own.

If I had listened to my body (gut) and my heart as well as my head, I would have made the right decision sooner and saved myself a lot of trouble. Now I apply total intelligence (body, heart, and head) when making decisions (more on this later). And when it comes to employees, I hire slowly and fire quickly.

Ironically, the situation with Doug ended up changing my life for the better. Because I agreed to work on the project for the medical device company, I commuted nearly an hour each direction, multiples days a week, to get to their offices. During my drive, I listened to *Mindset: The New Psychology of Success* by Carol Dweck, and it set me down the path toward my own awakening.

CULTURE MATTERS, TOO

In addition to the How, Why, What, and Which provided by the TriMetrix HD assessment, we look for people who match our core values—we need a cultural match, too. If you are the best technical person there is but don't match us culturally, you won't be a good fit. These are Alpine Security's core values and what we look for when considering whom to hire:

- Think flexibly to solve problems
- Find the opportunity in every situation
- Listen carefully, respond clearly
- Grow beyond your comfort zone
- Obsess over critical details
- Own the problem, find the solution
- Learn fast, learn often

I ask candidates technical questions, too, but only after I'm satisfied they have the people skills needed to succeed. Technical skills are skills I want to see in action. If a candidate says they can do something, I want to actually see them do it. (This is the best way to catch a paper tiger.) For example, if they say they can do a penetration test—which is an ethical hacking test—my team may create a scenario or test environment and watch them do it.

Technical skills are important, but I believe people skills are much more important to the success of cybersecurity professionals. That's why I screen for people skills first. Once you begin looking for people skills before technical skills, your hiring success improves.

DON'T GET TOO COMFORTABLE

Some of you don't think you have this problem. You already have someone you trust explicitly with your data—a fantastic CISO who knows what they're doing, communicates well, and has great people skills. If this is you, bravo.

However, I caution you not to get too comfortable. That star CISO or senior cybersecurity engineer could get a better offer from your competitor, turn in their resignation, and leave you high and dry, leaving you to quickly recruit someone new or promote from within.

As you likely know, recruiting in this competitive and expensive market will be tough, and promoting from within, especially if all of your CISO subordinates are hard to understand and work with, could be even worse. You need to prepare ahead of time and know how to screen for the best talent when the time comes—and it will—to hire someone new.

JOB HOPPERS

As a side note, I also screen for job hoppers and eliminate them from the candidate pool. (Job hoppers run rampant in the cybersecurity industry. Nine times out of ten, if someone has a history of job hopping every six to eighteen months, they're going to exhibit some of the issues and challenges I've been talking about [posturing, talking over people's heads, lack of perspective, etc.].)

Let me give you an example. One of my former employees, Doug, is currently on his seventh job in two and a half years, because as soon as things start to get hard, he leaves and goes somewhere new. He stopped working for me when our team, including me, kept butting heads with him and he couldn't handle it. The next thing I knew, he quit to go somewhere else.

Doug doesn't know he's the problem, nor does he recognize his job-hopping pattern. Whenever he is hired on someplace new, it starts off well, but soon "everyone is stupid," "they just don't get it," and "they aren't doing it right." So he leaves and goes to the next place. The common denominator in this equation is him.

Maybe if he learned how to better communicate with his management and peers, he could get them to listen to him and follow his advice. Instead, Doug doesn't change how he communicates or how he interacts with his peers; he simply blames them as the problem.

And he isn't the only one; I've seen this pattern time and again in my company and others. It's amazing how people like this still manage to get hired, but the industry claims to be so desperate for talent that guys like Doug get away with it.

WHAT ABOUT THE TALENT YOU ALREADY HAVE?

Recruiting for people skills over technical skills helps solve part of the problem, but you can't replace *everyone* on your team—not easily or affordably anyway. So what do you do with the people who already work in your company but who don't display the best people skills?

Many of the executives I work with have scores of cybersecurity and technical employees who already work for them. How do you address the issues I've been talking about with the employees you currently have, both to improve their current skills and to create a viable succession pipeline?

I would argue that it's much better to promote from within than to try and find someone new. They already know your culture and your clients. They're already familiar with the internal technical team. They can hit the ground running.

We, as leaders, need to feel comfortable with the risk. We need to trust whomever we chose to protect and secure our data. To that end, we need to teach them the people skills that will enable them to communicate effectively and work better with others to solve problems. Better communication begins with perspective.

PERSPECTIVE

Many technical people see the world from one vantage point: their own. And if you change it, they will likely freak out.

Seeing problems from the clients' perspectives is a critical aspect of cybersecurity, yet it isn't widely practiced. In order to find success in our industry—and in order to better safeguard sensitive data and devices—we need to help our technical employees bridge this gap between their perspective and management and client perspectives.

Perspective is everything, but when you see things from only one perspective (your own), anything else that doesn't align with that perspective is automatically wrong. For most technical people, it's harder to realize there may be alternatives because typically technical problems (and their solutions) are very black and white.

However, teams of individuals—with different mindsets and perspectives—can accomplish more than one person or a team full of people with the same perspective. Communication within and between teams is paramount to sharing those different perspectives.

FOLLOW THE STICKER TRAIL

Barefoot Wine's sales were slipping, so management called a company-wide meeting to brainstorm. The office manager came up with the idea to put big, round stickers on the grocery store floor that lead directly to their bottles on the shelves. Their customers no longer had to search high and low—all they had to do was follow the sticker trail.[9] The marketing team didn't come up with this idea; it was someone on the admin staff, which proves everyone has something to contribute.

KNOW YOUR WHY

What do you do if your existing team has trouble communicating and gaining that perspective? Go to the root of the problem—what motivates most of our technical staff to behave the way they do?

Leadership coach Simon Sinek gave a TED Talk about the importance of knowing your why and communicating it.[10] If someone on your technical staff doesn't understand why they're in cybersecurity or why it is important to them, they are setting themself up for failure. I always tell individuals entering cybersecurity to do it for the right reasons—to know their why. Once they do, their communication will improve (that has been my experience at least) and understanding different perspectives will become easier.

As the company leader, it's important for you to know your why,

---

9   Kim Orlesky, "06: How to Keep the Entrepreneurial Spirit Alive as You Grow with Barefoot Wine Founders Houlihan and Harvey," *Kim Orlesky* (blog), November 2, 2016, https://www.kimorlesky.com/blog/houlihan-and-harvey.

10   Simon Sinek, "How Great Leaders Inspire Action," TEDxPuget Sound, September 2009, https://www.ted.com/talks/simon_sinek_how_great_leaders_inspire_action?language=en.

too. Why do *you* come to work each day? What is *your* purpose for being there? How can you expect your team to know their why when you don't know your own?

Companies also must communicate their why to employees. Knowing the why behind things helps bring people together to accomplish something greater. It's a shift in mindset from:

"I do penetration testing" (the what).

To:

"I save lives" (the why) by "using my technical penetration testing skills" (the how) to "make medical devices secure from cybercriminals" (the *new* what).

It's necessary for everyone in the organization to know their why so cohesive collaboration can take place. When that happens, people work together more seamlessly and more problems get solved.

EXTREME OWNERSHIP

One of the most memorable stories from *Extreme Ownership* by Jocko Willink and Leif Babin highlights the following notion:

"There are no bad teams—only bad leaders."

Crew is an element of Navy SEAL training. In crew, each boat has seven rowers and one leader called the coxswain. The book features a story about two boats, each with a different coxswain and crew. One of the boats won every race, so the SEAL trainers decided to swap out coxswains.

Guess what happened? The winning coxswain, who had been traded to the losing team of rowers, won with them, too.[11]

Tony Robbins's "Six Basic Human Needs"

For a lot of people, knowing their why is easier said than done. Your technical staff is no exception. Many of them will struggle with this, but there are tools you can use to guide them.

I'm a big Tony Robbins fan. I've been to many of his events, including one in 2015 called "Date with Destiny" (DWD) that changed my life for the better. Tony Robbins is a coach and business and life strategist and has an excellent method for discovering your why. He coaches about six basic human needs, and how they each influence everything we do—they impact our feelings, thoughts, actions, and behaviors.

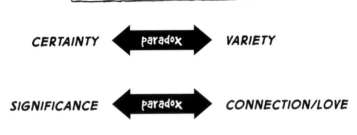

The Six Basic Human Needs.

The needs are broken out into two categories: the needs of the

---

11   Jocko Willink and Leif Babin, *Extreme Ownership: How U.S. Navy SEALs Lead and Win*, Kindle ed. (New York: St. Martin's, 2017), https://www.amazon.com/gp/product/B0739PYQSS.

personality and needs of the **spirit**. The first category, the needs of the personality, houses four of the most common needs, and most of us emphasize two of these four.

People typically need **certainty** in their life, which could equate to "I feel safe" or "I feel secure." Too much certainty can be boring, so another need is **variety/uncertainty**. Too much variety/uncertainty is for people who like drama and inconsistency. People also need to feel **significant**, be recognized, and perceived as important. They want to be notable. Finally, there's **connection/love**, the desire to feel close to someone else, the desire for relationships.

The paradox is that when things are too certain, we often do something to create variety (uncertainty). When there's too much uncertainty, we often crave certainty. It is also when we desire to be significant that we may diminish a partner or devalue a relationship. If we value connection/love too much, we may lose ourselves and what makes us unique and significant.

If you had to pick two of the four, which would you pick?

Most technical people would pick significance and certainty because they want to be the smartest person in the room. Everyone in their outside life thinks they're a genius, so their skillset makes them feel safe.

On the other hand, people who value love and connection may struggle in their day-to-day life if they're alone or unpartnered. Someone who craves uncertainty may find themselves in the middle of a lot of drama.

Like most technical people in cybersecurity, up until recently

I would have picked significance and certainty. Being the poor son of a drug-addicted mom, I never had any certainty growing up, so I craved it as an adult. I thought being the best at everything I did made me significant, too. I also didn't have any certainty because I didn't feel safe, so I built a fortress of technical skills to protect me.

What had worked for me growing up (that craving for significance and certainty) had stopped working for me as an adult, though. My need to be the best—also known as the smartest person in the room—blocked my ability to grow. Instead of being open to new ideas and seeing the world from the perspectives of other people, I was narrow-minded and viewed the world in black and white. This drove me to bully and talk over other people's heads. I thought I was smarter than everyone and didn't have any patience for anyone else's ideas. I had hit my peak in my career because I wasn't open to change, and I didn't really have a growth mindset, although I thought I did at the time.

Landmark Forum, DWD, and other events, along with a lot of books, courses, reflection, and soul searching, allowed me to recognize that what had motivated me up until that point in my life was now holding me back. I discovered I wanted to get more comfortable with *un*certainty, not for the sake of drama but for the sake of growth. I also realized I had been sacrificing connection/love (maybe because there's a lot of uncertainty in relationships) and no longer wanted to—I wanted to embrace it.

Transformation is a journey, though—I want to make that clear. It doesn't happen at a single event or after you read one book. It takes practice, hard work, and time.

GAMING AND THE SIX HUMAN NEEDS

Most of us want to do things that satisfy as many of our human needs as possible. If a job doesn't fit those needs, for example, we probably won't be fulfilled.

Gaming satisfies all six human needs. That's one of the main reasons why **Massive Multiplayer Online Role-Playing Games (MMOPRGS)** like World of Warcraft or EverQuest are so addictive.

- **Certainty** because players understand the world and how to interact with it. They also may be a member of a guild, which provides stability.
- **Variety/uncertainty** because when you kill things, the result is always different. *Will the supercool sword "drop" this time?*
- **Significance** because you are part of a guild and you can earn/buy items for your character. You can personalize it.
- **Connection/love** because you play with your virtual guild members. You form bonds as you play the game.
- **Growth** because you constantly earn new skills and "level up."
- **Contribution** because you are contributing to your guild's success.

Games hit all six human needs, but everyone is motivated differently. It's the job of leadership to understand these differences and harness them appropriately.

Growth and Contribution

I originally mentioned there were *six* human needs, but I've given you only four. The other two are the needs of the spirit, **growth** and **contribution**, which are typically only achievable with expanded awareness and consciousness. This is something that takes time because to get there, you've got to flip the switch, evolve, and mature. If you've valued significance and certainty your whole life like me, perhaps it's time to give connection/ love and uncertainty a whirl. If you typically say no, it's time to start saying yes. That's how you grow and expand and eventually contribute, either to your job, the greater good, or both.

My COO—also known as Captain Phasma of the 501st Legion— started out craving connection/love and certainty (I think that's why she likes "The Dark Side" and the Republic—it's all about law and order, unlike the Rebel Alliance). The relationships she has with her peers, subordinates, and Star Wars troop are rich and full.

She has never been a fan of uncertainty (because to her it equals surrender), but through a lot of personal work, she "embraced" it. She demonstrated a desire to grow (and still does), and by welcoming something she once used to avoid, she deepened her people skills, improved her communication with her peers, and broadened her perspective. Now she's one of the best at what she does. Her problem-solving skills in our field are top notch, not because of the technical skills she learned but because of her refined *people* skills.

Refining those skills took a lot of effort, but she was committed to it. Through weekly and monthly sessions, I coached her on leadership and embracing uncertainty, *but her growth is entirely her own.* She worked day and night to discover her why and push through her barriers to welcome the thing that scared her the most—uncertainty. Now she can focus her energy on growth and contribution, the ultimate goal.

And she's a better (and more effective) leader because of it.

It has been my experience that successful cybersecurity leaders (and technical employees in general) are the leaders who value growth and contribution. Their perspectives are broader and their communication is more effective.

How do *you* as a leader learn to value growth and contribution? How do you coach your technical team to do the same?

We focus on people skills. It's time to move into the Secure Methodology.

CHAPTER 2

▪ ▪ ▪

THE SECURE METHODOLOGY

If everyone is thinking alike, then somebody isn't thinking.

—GEORGE S. PATTON

When I first started my company, I considered bringing on a partner. Doug (the job hopper from chapter 1) was the smartest guy I knew (at least I thought so at the time), and I believed he would be a genuine asset to the team. I thought he would help move the company forward.

I hired him as a technical executive and planned to make him a partner in my company, but contrary to the COO, aka Captain Phasma, soon discovered he couldn't (or wouldn't) develop his people skills. It was clear to me that Doug had created his own view of the world and expected everyone else to operate within his parameters. As a result, he wasn't communicating clearly or connecting with the staff. Although technically competent, he was failing as a company leader.

When I tried to hold him accountable, Doug quit. He had always been the smartest person in the room and couldn't take the criticism, so instead of trying to improve, he decided to move on. That was three years ago, and Doug has had seven different jobs since. That tells me that he hasn't changed at all. He continues to think everyone is programmed the same way he is, and when he realizes they aren't (and that they won't adopt his way of thinking), he gets frustrated and leaves the company. He repeats this process over, and over, and over again...and never gets off the hamster wheel. He's aggravated and unhappy, yet he expects everyone else to change instead.

WHOSE DIGITAL PROTRACTOR IS BIGGER?

Doug refused to develop people skills and bragged many times that being "intellectually superior" allowed him to treat people however he wanted. He believed he was the smartest person in the room and had the right to "walk all over them."

However, Doug also lived in fear. He was terrified of being intellectually *inferior* and that someone else might have a bigger digital protractor and somehow prove they were smarter.

Real intelligence is a sign of how well you live your life. It isn't measured by your IQ. There's a general notion that if you have a high IQ, you're incapable of relating to people—this is an excuse that only justifies the behavior. What does the ability to determine patterns in an IQ test have to do with people, relationships, and life? A high IQ has been used to justify a lack of EQ (emotional intelligence), and it has ultimately led to problems in the cybersecurity industry.

RUNNING ON A HAMSTER WHEEL

Sometimes we get so caught up with "life" that we don't realize we aren't getting anywhere.

I was running on my own hamster wheel for a while before I realized it. When I quit my corporate job, there wasn't an immediate switch that flipped or anything. It wasn't as if I completely ignored the importance of people skills one day and then fully embodied them the next. It took me a while to realize I was the source of my own problems, because I was chasing significance and happiness, an endless and exhausting pursuit. It took me a while to step off the hamster wheel and stop running.

When I started Alpine Security, things began to change but quite *slowly*. Starting (and growing) a cybersecurity services business was much more difficult than I thought it would be. I found myself having to manage everything and realized the negative implications of a lack of people skills. I started listening in on phone calls my technical team members were having with clients, and I noticed patterns in their communication style (or lack thereof) and behaviors. I noticed a lot of insecurity, fear, and posturing.

During my observations, I also realized how consequential my team's general lack of people skills were. I was the business owner and funded everything. I had cashed in my life savings to start my business and assumed all the risk if it failed. The consequences were very real to me, and it was this new awareness that convinced me to finally change.

Then a light bulb went off. As I became aware of these patterns in my team, I became aware of them in myself. (To this day, I still believe in self-awareness and self-improvement. I know I have many, *many* improvements to make in all areas of my life, people skills included.)

After that, I started seeing these patterns in cybersecurity and in IT *everywhere*, and I realized it was a major problem for me, my peers, clients, and the industry. It's like when you buy a new red car. Suddenly, you start to see red cars everywhere. That's how it was for me. Everywhere I looked, I saw the same problems. They all stemmed from poor people skills, and the cybersecurity industry's acceptance and tolerance of these poor people skills is causing us to lose the cybersecurity war. It goes along with the notion of "you get what you tolerate."

The brain is programmed to find what you're looking for, which ties into one of the fundamental concepts in *Think and Grow Rich* by Napoleon Hill.

"Whatever the mind can conceive and believe, it can achieve."

If you think the world is out to get you, for example, your brain will find ways to support this idea. On the other hand, if you think the world is a great place and people are fundamentally good, that's what you'll see. Without the right mindset, there is no awareness of what's possible and of what opportunities exist.

This shift in perspective is everything and can have massive impact, both on your life and the lives of your technical staff. As a leader, it's just as important for you to have the right mindset as it is for your team.

A LIMITED EDITION M THEORY

In 2007, a friend of mine bought a new, limited edition Toyota Corolla Matrix M-Theory. Supposedly, only 2,500 of these were produced.[12] It was Speedway Blue, and it was great. The two of us would take it on road trips and to triathlons because it could easily fit all of our equipment.

The funny thing was, even though it was a "limited edition" vehicle, we saw it on the road *everywhere*. We'd see M-Theory Matrixes parked at gas stations and restaurants and passing us on the road. If my buddy didn't own the car, we never would have noticed them.

REPROGRAM YOURSELF

The problems I saw in cybersecurity were everywhere, but I also saw a glimmer of hope for resolving them and making the industry better and more, well, secure at the same time. That glimmer is the Secure Methodology.

At the beginning of this book, I told you the methodology isn't

---

12 Joel Arrelano, "Toyota Matrix M-Theory Package Announced," *Autoblog*, August 1, 2006, https://www.autoblog.com/2006/08/01/toyota-matrix-m-theory-package-announced/.

a silver bullet. Following the steps outlined in the rest of this book won't change you or your team overnight.

The methodology is a *journey* because changing and improving behavior takes time. I mentioned a "light bulb going off," but that was the beginning—the light shines brightly on the work I have to do. I'm still a work in progress, and I probably always will be. Deep work takes time because we have to reprogram our brains, and that isn't something we can rush, especially if the patterns have existed for a long time.

What am I talking about? Stick with me.

People have routine behaviors and patterns that, according to NLP, run inside your mind all the time, almost like a computer program. You don't realize they're running, but they are. These patterns dictate how you interact with the world and with your-self—how you *think* about yourself, what you *tell* yourself, how *happy* you are, and more.

Let's say your mom always used to get on your case to make the bed. It was something that she nagged you about constantly. Now as an adult, every time you're asked to make the bed, you get irritable because it kicks off a program in your brain you established when you were a kid. If you took a step back, you could probably predict everything that happens next. These are bad habits, or programs, that are running in your brain. We need to "hack" our brains and reprogram them to get rid of these bad habits.

NEURAL PATHWAYS AND NEURAL PLASTICITY

Neural pathways comprise **neurons** connected by **dendrites** (neuron "branches" that reach out toward other neurons to exchange data) and are created in the brain based on habits and behaviors. The more often these habits and behaviors are used, the stronger these pathways become. They eventually turn into neural superhighways. This is why bad habits are hard to break and good ones are even harder to form. To grow and change, we need to destroy the bad-habit superhighways (ruts) and create *new* pathways, which may start out as bumpy dirt roads.

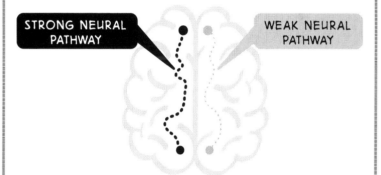

STRONG NEURAL PATHWAY

WEAK NEURAL PATHWAY

Old habits have strong neural pathways. New habits have weak ones. The more we use a pathway, the stronger it gets. The less we use a pathway, the weaker it gets.

Many people think these neural pathways are locked in place and they are hardwired to think and act the way they do. This isn't true, though. Thanks to **neural plasticity**, our brains really *do* have the capacity to change. We can rewire our brains and replace the old programs (pathways) with the new ones. We can reprogram our brains.

We are basically caught in an "if, then, else" loop. (This is cybersecurity, robot talk for all you nontechnical readers.)

If this happens, *then* do this, *else* do that.

Our brains are not much different than computers. We like to think we are different and that our behavior is unpredictable, but we are *very* predictable. Take a second and think about the last time you were "triggered." What happened? Did you have much control over how you responded, or did you go on autopilot?

(The last time you were told to make the bed, did you have rational conversation about it, or did you get irritable and snap like you always do?)

We've all become conditioned to think the only decision-making cells in our bodies are in our brains, but our entire body is made up of cells and they all communicate with each other. We have a neurological system that stores and processes information faster than we can consciously rationalize, and most people dismiss it.

WHERE ARE MEMORIES STORED?

Our memories aren't just stored in our brain. They are stored in our entire body, including the heart. In *The Heart's Code: Tapping the Wisdom and Power of Our Heart Energy*, author Paul P. Pearsall tells the story of an eight-year-old girl who received a heart transplant from another little girl (age ten) who was murdered.

After the transplant, the eight-year-old with the new heart started having nightmares about the man who murdered the donor. The nightmares were vivid and detailed—the little girl was able to describe the clothes the killer wore, the murder weapon, and the time and location of the murder. The little girl's mother reported all of this to the police, who were able to identify and arrest the donor's killer. Memories don't live only in the brain.

In order to get rid of these deeply embedded patterns and behaviors, you have to dig down deep into this network and reprogram yourself.

LEAD WITH TOTAL INTELLIGENCE

When it comes to technical people, which patterns and behaviors should we try to reprogram first?

Most technical people lead and interact with the world with their heads. They tend to be logical and left-brained and see the world in black and white—remember the 1s and 0s story? Technical people tend to think everyone thinks the same way they do, too. And they believe their approach to problems is the best.

Technical people also lead with their heads because it's easy and what comes naturally to them. When they lead with their heads, they can focus on what makes the most logical sense. They don't have to worry about "feelings" or "instincts." However, this way of thinking has led to problems in the cybersecurity industry—many people in technical roles posture and bully because of it, which inhibits communication and prevents problem solving.

We need our technical employees to lead with *more* than their heads. We need them to lead with their hearts and bodies as well. We need them to pay attention to their feelings, listen to their instincts, and spend less time thinking. **Total intelligence** is the ability to lead with your head, your heart, *and* your body. (A lot of people refer to this last one as a "gut feeling" even though the associated sensations are most often felt throughout the *entire* body, like a chill down the spine or arm hair standing on end.)

We need our technical team to lead with total intelligence—their heads, hearts, *and* bodies. This requires self-awareness, which is difficult for a lot of people, technical or not. Assessment tests can help with self-awareness. They aren't 100 percent accurate, but I'm a fan of them because they give you an idea of who you are, how you see yourself, and how others see you.

The Enneagram[13] is a test that helps with self-awareness. It uses the body (instinctive), heart (feeling), and head (thinking) as elements of the assessment to summarize key points about you and provide you with a bunch of personal information to make you more self-aware and ultimately help you.[14]

I took a course on the Enneagram and did the assessment. I believe all leaders and their team should take the assessment as well. I'm an Enneagram Type 7 (Enthusiastic Visionary). Here is a summary of my results, which are spookily accurate:

Perspective: The future is full of thrilling possibilities.

Focus: Your energy is centered on what excites you—you focus on your wants and needs, as well as your interests. Your spotlight is on the future, not the past.

Fears: Limits and restrictions; pain, irritation, and discomfort; not living life to the fullest.

---

13   "Your Invitation to Try the Most Accurate and In-Depth Enneagram Report Available," *Ian Morgan Cron*, accessed November 13, 2020, https://ianmorgancron.com/assessment.

14   "How the Enneagram System Works," The Enneagram Institute, accessed November 13, 2020, https://www.enneagraminstitute.com/how-the-enneagram-system-works.

Internal Dialogue: What I want, I deserve. What's next? I will move forward. I must be free.

Contributions: Happiness, generosity, independence, appreciation.

Shortcomings: Greed and overindulgence for new experiences, sustained dissatisfaction, shallow attachments/lack of intimacy.[15]

Total intelligence means having deep conversations, being vulnerable and uncomfortable. It means being compassionate and engaging in open communication. To lead with your head, your heart, *and* your body, you have to put yourself into someone else's shoes and really try to see and understand things from their perspective. This isn't only about logic or empathy or "gut instinct" (you know, the hairs on your arm that stand on end, or the shiver that runs up and down your spine); it's about using all three. Many technical people ignore their hearts and their bodies and focus on only their heads.

I'm not saying that all decisions should be heart led—total intelligence means listening to *more than one* (and ideally all three—head, heart, and body) when making decisions. I've analyzed my own decisions over the past five or six years, and every time I made a strictly logical decision (as opposed to listening to my heart and my body as well), 90 percent of those decisions were wrong. If I had made decisions using my total intelligence, I would have been 90 percent *right*. My head told me Doug wasn't right for the organization. My body felt it, too. I wanted to help Doug, though, so I ignored them and listened

---

15   Report snippet from the Enneagram assessment.

to my heart; but as I found out, following one area without consideration of the others is a recipe for disaster.

Today, I try to lead with total intelligence (the head, the heart, and the body). I will think the problem through logically, but if my heart or my body is strongly telling me to do something—even against all logic—I'll listen. This is not as simple as it sounds because technical people tend to place more emphasis on their head space.

To beat cybercriminals, cybersecurity experts need to develop their people skills and use their total intelligence. They need to be reprogrammed to lead with their hearts and bodies, too, not just their heads. Fully using all of our faculties (types of intelligence) will help us be better equipped to fight the cyberwar.

I'm not suggesting we replace logic completely—logic should still be applied to problem solving. What I *am* saying is that logic, emotion, and instinct should be complementary. If a technical employee can see the problem through the eyes of their client, as well as understand the problem logically, they'll provide better solutions. This applies to working as a team, too.

If there's a problem internally, I want to know where the people involved are coming from. If they're asking for help, I want to know why. I want to know what their world looks like because it helps me provide simple solutions that will actually help them solve their problems and achieve their goals. So I ask questions.

ASK THE RIGHT QUESTIONS

Questions are important, but if you want insightful answers, you have to ask the right ones. Like anything else, this is a skill that takes practice to master.

Generally speaking, "what" and "how" questions are better than "why" questions. "Why" questions typically put people on the defensive.

Total intelligence takes advanced people skills. It takes heightened awareness, a growth mindset, acknowledgment, and the right language. It means hyperfocus, empathy, and an infinite quest for improvement. This is not a journey for those who value comfort and the status quo. We've been following the status quo in cybersecurity for years, and it's not working.

How do we get our technical employees to embrace total intelligence? How do we get them to more effectively fight the cybersecurity war?

The Secure Methodology.

THE SECURE METHODOLOGY

To win the war, we need to get our technical people to strengthen their people skills and lead with their hearts. If we can do that, their communication skills will naturally improve, and as I've previously stated, *open communication allows us to solve problems and commit to fixing them.*

The Secure Methodology is a step-by-step guide designed to show you exactly how to jump-start your technical staff's people skills in order to have open, honest, and effective communication. It promotes more in-depth understanding. When everyone in your organization is on the same page and working together to fight cybercrime, your chances of winning will improve.

The method includes seven different steps. Here is a high-level overview of each of them.

1. AWARENESS

There are two aspects to awareness. The first is *self*-awareness, which is understanding the behaviors you're in control of. You impact the world around you, so you should be aware of your interactions within it. This could be a smile, a frown, or a profanity-filled rant. Whatever it is, your actions *will* impact someone, and you should be aware of it. Many technical people (and people in general) struggle with self-awareness because we tend to fill our lives with stimuli (music, TV, games, social media, etc.) and make little time for reflection. As a leader, you may struggle with it, too. You may not even be aware of how you are "showing up." The energy you bring to a meeting or to a room will have an impact on your team.

There is also the awareness of others to consider here. Being aware of only your own actions is self-centered and doesn't lend well to problem solving. For example, maybe a coworker is having a bad day (for whatever reason) and has been crying at their desk. Don't make an assumption. Assumptions come from our own experience and often cloud the truth. Rather than make an assumption, it's better to ask your coworker how they're feeling. If you're aware of the reason behind their tears, you may not be so hard on them when they tell you they're going to be late on a deadline. If you're unaware, you're likely to get more confrontational and heated, which will only make matters worse. Awareness means being aware of others just as much as it means being aware of ourselves.

2. MINDSET

There are two different types of mindset—growth and fixed. If you have a fixed mindset, you believe things are the way they are and that you are incapable of change. For example, a lot of technical people will say, "I'm not good with people." This is a fixed mindset. Someone with a growth mindset will say, "I have challenges with people, but I can get better." They know they can learn and change.

Many technical employees believe they have a growth mindset because they are capable of learning new technologies, but this isn't about hard skills; this is about *soft* skills. Soft skills are much harder to master than hard skills. Having a growth mindset means belief in the ability to change (and master) soft skills. A lot of people confuse mindset with attitude, but they aren't the same. They go hand in hand, but attitude is a subset of mindset. If I try something new and it doesn't work out, my mindset will determine the attitude I have about it.

If you don't have the right mindset, you're not going to change. This goes for both you and your technical staff. *You* have to believe your team is capable of change just as much as they do. You also need to be committed to change. This, too, requires the right mindset. Many people (technical people included) want to change but give up when it gets too hard. Real change doesn't happen overnight, and change requires commitment. If you want to change the people skills or your technical staff, you and your staff need to be committed to that change.

3. ACKNOWLEDGMENT

There are a few things to keep in mind when it comes to acknowledgment. First, our technical employees should focus on the power of self-acknowledgment. Many people on our technical team think they aren't good enough, but this is simply not the case. They aren't broken and they don't need to be fixed. That isn't what the methodology is about. Your technical team *is* enough and whole the way they are, and when we encourage them to acknowledge that, their egos start to dissolve, and posturing goes away.

Acknowledgment is also essential to successfully leading a team. If you are supervising someone and want them to change their behavior at work, you need to first acknowledge everything they've *already* accomplished. Most technical people (except for the paper tigers) worked hard to get where they are and develop their skills. If you, as a leader, don't acknowledge everything they've already achieved, they will likely shut down and be less likely to change.

You also need to acknowledge your technical employees when they make positive changes to their behavior, and that acknowledgment needs to be genuine and sincere. You want their people skills to improve, and when they do, even slightly, you need to acknowledge their success. Otherwise, how will they know if they're on the right track? When training a new puppy, you give them a treat every time they do something (e.g., goes to the bathroom outside). Positive reinforcement in this scenario is needed in order to get the puppy to permanently adapt its behavior. I'm not trying to relate your technical staff to dogs; I'm just saying that positive change of any kind should be acknowledged and even rewarded. Leading with a carrot is generally more effective than leading with a stick.

4. COMMUNICATION

Communication boils down to the way we interact and the language we use. Many studies show that when it comes down to communication, people comprehend only about 7 percent of the words they hear. Most of their comprehension comes from tonality (38 percent) and body language (55 percent).[16] Communication isn't just the words we use—it's *how* we say them and the positions of our bodies when we do. Many technical people miss these nuances and focus only on words. This is problematic and leads to breakdowns in communication across the team. Technical people need to understand how they communicate; leaders and trainers should understand their own communication patterns, too.

MEHRABIAN'S 7-38-55 THEORY OF COMMUNICATIONS

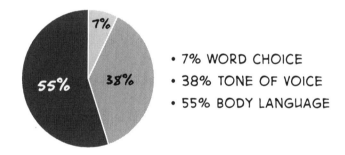

- 7% WORD CHOICE
- 38% TONE OF VOICE
- 55% BODY LANGUAGE

The words you choose have less of an impact on communication than tone of voice and body language.

If the stat I gave you in the last paragraph leads you to think language is unimportant, think again. Specific word choice is also critical to communication because it can provide insight into the other person's state of mind. For example, I was speaking to an executive about a problem he was having, and he used very

---

16   Wikipedia, s.v. "Albert Mehrabian," last modified September 23, 2020, https://en.wikipedia.org/wiki/Albert_Mehrabian.

physical language such as "shouldering," "derailing," "falling to the floor," and "pushing a rock up a hill." This specific language told me he was really struggling with the issue, which allowed me as his leader and coach to lend additional support (both tactically and emotionally) when needed to solve the problem. Sometimes, and probably most times, the problem exists only in our heads.

5. MONOTASKING

I am a big believer in concentrated work, and I believe this is true for most people. Most of us want to do quality work and don't want to be distracted constantly because it's unproductive. *Quality* work requires focusing on one task at a time, or monotasking—the opposite of the ever-so-popular multitasking. Most people think they get more done when they multitask, but the opposite is true. When you give attention to one task for a full hour, you'll accomplish more (probably ten times more) in that hour than you would if you had broken the project down to shorter increments scattered throughout the day. It's much harder to get as much accomplished this way, and it's almost impossible to create anything of quality. Could this be another battle lost in the cybersecurity war?

We often get caught up thinking we need to respond immediately to everything—to phone calls, emails, text messages, social media invites, and so on—and we end up playing a supporting role in someone else's movie, rather than starring in our own. We respond to everyone else's demands on our time; we make little progress in our own lives. We may be busy, but we aren't necessarily productive. Monotasking also means reserving concentrated time to work on you.

Most technical people don't know how to monotask. (Do you?) If you don't believe me, just look around your office. How many people do you see surrounded by multiple monitors? And how many of these people are technical? Being surrounded by six monitors can't possibly be a distraction-free environment. Is the point of all those monitors that the person in front of them can work on multiple projects at the same time? Monotasking doesn't mean working on the same task for eighty hours straight, but it does mean focusing on one thing (without distractions) for at least hour chunks, longer if that works for you.

6. EMPATHY

A lot of technical people assume they're the only ones with challenges and that everyone else has it easy. However, this is self-centered (some would even say narcissistic) thinking and can only lead to problems. Being self-absorbed (versus connecting with people) has been tied to depression.[17] A lack of connection has also been tied to addiction,[18] and there's a lot of *dis*connection in the world today. Should it really be a surprise that so many people struggle with empathy? Shouldn't you, as a leader, be empathetic to this struggle?

---

17 Leon F. Seltzer, "Self-Absorption: The Root of All Psychological Evil?" *Psychology Today*, August 24, 2016, https://www.psychologytoday.com/us/blog/evolution-the-self/201608/self-absorption-the-root-all-psychological-evil.

18 Robert Weiss, "The Opposite of Addiction Is Connection," *Psychology Today*, September 30, 2015, https://www.psychologytoday.com/us/blog/love-and-sex-in-the-digital-age/201509/the-opposite-addiction-is-connection.

RAT PARK

Rat Park was a series of drug addiction studies that took place in the late 1970s by Bruce K. Alexander and his colleagues at Simon Fraser University in British Columbia.[19] (Results were published between 1978 and 1981.)

In the experiment, a group of rats were given two drinking bottles to choose from—one was filled with water and the other with morphine. When the rats were all together (running, eating, procreating), they rarely went for the morphine. The connectedness removed the desire to get high all the time. When a rat was alone, on the other hand, it *always* went for the morphine until it eventually overdosed.

Like rats, humans need connection.[20]

When interacting with others, self-centered thinking often leads to quick and incorrect conclusions. This impacts communication and the ability to problem solve because when we jump to conclusions, we don't give the other person the benefit of the doubt—we don't put ourselves in their shoes and see the world from their perspective. Other people have their own challenges to deal with, and chances are, the person in question doesn't *want* to behave that way. Chances are, there is a perfectly good explanation for their behavior. When we understand where someone is coming from, we lead with our hearts, rather than our heads, which typically generates better results.

---

19   Wikipedia, s.v. "Rat Park," last modified October 30, 2020, https://en.wikipedia.org/wiki/Rat_Park.

20   Johann Hari, "Everything You Think You Know about Addiction Is Wrong," TEDGlobalLondon, June 2015, https://www.ted.com/talks/johann_hari_everything_you_think_you_know_about_addiction_is_wrong?language=en.

7. KAIZEN

True growth and contribution, the ultimate goal of the Secure Methodology, is only possible through constant and never-ending improvement. Once we establish a new process or practice, we need to examine it and fine-tune it continuously. This practice could be internal—a daily habit or a daily "morning routine." It could also be external—like a process at work or our procedures for detecting cybercriminals on our networks.

"Progress equals happiness." It also leads to contribution. You can't contribute unless you grow, and you can't grow unless you practice kaizen. To get better, we have to *be* better. People who progress in life are happier than people who are stagnant. Think about it. If you make the same paycheck today as you did ten years ago, how would you feel about that? What if your marriage has regressed instead of progressed? What if you have more data breaches today than you had last year?

Progress equals happiness. As humans, as organizations, we feel most alive and happy when we are progressing in something we care about. When we are stagnant or stuck, we aren't happy. Kaizen is about continuous improvement, which equals progress. Employees who feel progress and are happy are more engaged.

Growth and progress lead to happiness. It also leads to contribution. You can't contribute unless you grow, and you can't grow unless you practice kaizen. When you try something new, you're not going to get it right the first, second, third time. Kaizen is the understanding, and even encouragement of this. To get desirable results, you have to practice. You can't just dabble. Mastery is a journey and takes time. Life is uncertain, and we need to embrace it so we can make constant improvement. This ties back to the very beginning of the methodology: awareness and a growth mindset.

These seven steps are a kaizen of their own; learning them and working toward mastery is an ongoing practice. And as you do, keep in mind the steps all weave together. A fair amount of information applies to each of them.

NLP PRESUPPOSITIONS

NLP presuppositions are an unbiased and compelling set of beliefs one can incorporate into one's life. I use the presuppositions as a reminder to check my perspective and think about things differently. I also use them to help guide me through the Secure Methodology.

There are fourteen presuppositions:

1. **Respect for the other person's model of the world.**
2. **Behavior and change are to be evaluated in terms of context and ecology.**
3. **Resistance is a sign of a lack of rapport.**
   (There are no resistant clients, only inflexible communicators. Effective communicators accept and utilize all communication present to them.)
4. **People are not their behaviors.**
   (Accept the person; change the behavior.)
5. **Everyone is doing the best they can with the resources they have available.**
   (Behavior is geared for adaptation, and present behavior is the best choice available. Every behavior is motivated by a positive intent.)
6. **Calibrate on behavior.**
   (The most important information about a person is that person's behavior.)

7. **The map is not the territory.**
    (The words we use are NOT the event or the item they represent.)
8. **You are in charge of your mind and therefore your results.**
    (I am also in charge of my mind and therefore my results.)
9. **People have all the resources they need to succeed and to achieve their desired outcomes.**
    (There are no unresourceful people, only unresourceful states.)
10. **All procedures should increase wholeness.**
11. **There is ONLY feedback!**
    (There is no failure, only feedback.)
12. **The meaning of communication is the response you get.**
13. **The law of requisite variety.**
    (The system/person with the most flexibility of behavior will control the system.)
14. **All procedures should be designed to increase choice.**[21]

The book isn't about NLP but rather points to it as a useful tool. Each of these presuppositions can be applied to at least one step in the Secure Methodology used to help develop better habits and behaviors.

NLP is technical in nature—it is literally about how the brain is programmed. NLP is one tool you can use to update that program, but it certainly is not the *only* way to accomplish those goals. It's a method I find extremely useful, so I compiled a list of applicable presuppositions for every step in the methodology.

SUCCESS VERSUS FULFILLMENT

There is a big difference between success and fulfillment. Elvis Presley is an excellent example of this. (I've been to Graceland, and the property is fascinating. The Jungle Room might be my

---

21 Terry Elston, "NLP Practitioner: Presuppositions of NLP," NLP World, accessed November 13, 2020, https://www.nlpworld.co.uk/nlp-presuppositions/.

favorite.) Elvis was "successful" but not fulfilled, so he took prescription barbiturates until his heart gave out.[22] Many people are highly successful but overwhelmingly unfulfilled. I was one of them, which is why I made the change.

Today, I'm not nearly as "successful" as I once was, but I'm certainly more fulfilled. That fulfillment has led to my growth and contribution (and winning the internal war), which are more important to me than titles or a bank full of gold. Chasing significance and happiness is a never-ending pursuit.

Typically, the people who are successful and fulfilled are also contributing and growing. That's the point of the Secure Methodology—to teach your technical staff the people skills they need to grow and contribute to the overall betterment of the cybersecurity industry and their lives.

Isn't that what we *all* want? To improve the quality of the industry and win the war (both the cybersecurity war and the war within ourselves)? The Secure Methodology is a surefire way to ignite the people skills of your technical team so we can beat cybercriminals and win the war.

And who knows? Maybe you'll improve some of your own, too.

In the chapters that follow, I will outline each step in the method and the steps both you and your technical team need to take to achieve success. Without further ado, let's get started with the first step, *Awareness.*

---

22   History.com Editors, "Elvis Presley Dies," *History*, accessed November 13, 2020, https://www.history.com/this-day-in-history/elvis-presley-dies.

CHAPTER 3

■ ■ ■

STEP I: AWARENESS

What is necessary to change a person is to change his awareness of himself.

—ABRAHAM MASLOW

A good friend of mine used to be addicted to SimCity. For those of you who haven't heard of it, it's a computer and mobile game that simulates real life. In SimCity, you can customize your digital world any way you'd like. You build houses and communities and, if you want, communicate with other players live online.

The game has been around for ages, and my buddy played it for years, but one day, a stark realization hit him. He was playing the game, and his digital room in his digital house was a mess. So he decided to clean it up. He was just about to empty his *virtual* trash can when his own overflowing, *real-life* trash caught his eye. He had been so busy worried about emptying the virtual trash can that he had completely neglected the real one.

That was a defining moment for my friend. As soon as he was aware that his real-life responsibilities had suffered because he was too busy focusing on his digital ones, he quit the game and never looked back.

NLP PRESUPPOSITIONS FOR AWARENESS

- **Respect for the other person's model of the world.**
- **People are not their behaviors.**
  (Accept the person; change the behavior.)
- **Everyone is doing the best they can with the resources they have available.**
  (Behavior is geared for adaptation, and present behavior is the best choice available. Every behavior is motivated by a positive intent.)
- **Calibrate on behavior.**
  (The most important information about a person is that person's behavior.)
- **The map is not the territory.**
  (The words we use are NOT the event or the item they represent.)
- **People have all the resources they need to succeed and to achieve their desired outcomes.**
  (There are no unresourceful people, only unresourceful states.)
  Awareness and Blind Spots, a Love Story

All human beings have blind spots. We all have behavior patterns we're *completely unaware of* yet repeat over and over again. These are typically behaviors that inhibit our growth and stand in the way of our success.

For a long time, my friend was unaware of his behavior. He had a blind spot. He was spending so much time living in his digital world that he neglected the real-life one. His SimCity habits impacted his life in a negative way, and he was completely unaware of it.

Blind spots are programmed in the unconscious mind—that's why we're unaware of them. Each blind spot is a program that runs in the background of your mind. (This ties into NLP, which we'll get into toward the end of the chapter.) Habits are programmed in the unconscious mind, too, so it's natural to see how our blind spots influence our habits. Bad habits form because blind spots exist, and neuropathways become super-highways, also known as ruts.

Is it possible to identify our blind spots?

Yes, and it's essential that we do. It's difficult and takes a lot of deep work, but our blind spots are at the root of most of our problems. The sooner we recognize them, the sooner we can start to break the bad habits they've helped form.

Because NLP comprises how *all* the senses work together to communicate, we can begin observing our reactions (head, heart, and body) to situations or conversations to increase awareness and uncover our blind spots. It isn't just the words we use. For example, if our pulse quickens and we have a panic attack every time we hear sirens, we're running a program (often malware) in the back of our mind that has an auditory trigger and creates a physical response.

Once we identify our blind spots, we can then choose whether or not to keep the program running. Some programs are harder to uninstall than others, but if we can recognize a program and become aware of that program's existence, it's our *choice* to keep that program running. That means, if we're aware of how we communicate with ourselves and with others, we can identify those programs that hinder us and change them to help us improve our lives.

THE IMPACT ON CYBERSECURITY

Our technical employees' lack of awareness and their inability to recognize their blind spots is one of the reasons why we're losing the cybersecurity war. Not only are they lacking in self-awareness, but they're also often lacking in awareness comprehension—many technical people don't understand their behavior and how it influences the world around them.

It doesn't matter which awareness ailment your technical staff suffers from—a lack of awareness leads to problems in the industry because it negatively impacts relationships and job quality. It's hard to work with others to win the cybersecurity war when the lack of awareness interferes with problem solving and teamwork.

RELATIONSHIPS

A lack of awareness causes incessant issues at work. It particularly creates problems with coworkers. Let me start off with an example.

Every Monday, I typically go over "the numbers" with my team. "The numbers" are sales (revenue) for the previous week compared to where we are expected to be, our projections, along with our minimums. I believe in a transparent organization so we can all band together and unite under a common goal. I remember one Monday in particular when I had to report we were 40 percent behind on revenue for the month. I told my team we could make it up, but everyone would have to work hard and really push to complete billable milestones for new projects, as well as complete existing projects under budget.

After the meeting was over, I was approached privately by one of the attendees, Karen, a technical employee. She wanted to talk to me about a raise.

I was shocked. I had just informed everyone that we were behind on our gross revenue goals for the month, yet she wanted *more money*. Her lack of awareness was staggering. She obviously hadn't spent any time putting herself in my shoes to see the situation from my perspective. My company is solely funded; I don't have any investors—it's just me. If I can't make payroll because I'm 40 percent behind on revenue for the month, I have to cash in my investments to cover it, cut my salary, get a loan, or beg friends and family for money.

I explained this to Karen, but it was as if she didn't hear me. Instead of recognizing her own error, she switched gears and started to blame our sales team.

"Well, if sales would do their job, we wouldn't be in this position," she said.

"Why are you so quick to blame them? Do you know how difficult their job is?"

"It can't be as hard as mine."

One of my biggest pet peeves is entitlement—people who expect to earn something for nothing. I don't have patience for people who don't want to risk anything yet expect to reap the rewards.

"Should I tie your salary to performance metrics, too, and start you out at a base salary of $2,000 a month? Are you okay living off your performance the way sales lives off commissions?"

Karen just looked at me, with a blank expression on her face. She wasn't trying to understand a word of what I was saying. She was simply listening for something to agree with, and when she didn't hear it, she turned around and walked out of the conference room.

A lack of awareness impacts relationships because it creates animosity and resentment among team members. It also causes a breakdown in communication. How can technical people work with others to solve problems in cybersecurity if they don't get along with each other?

JOB QUALITY

A lack of awareness also impacts your technical staff's job quality because it hinders their ability to communicate with clients. This can often result in dissatisfaction or situations where you will need to do "damage control." For example, we had an employee who communicated in short bursts of facts.

"We need this."

"We need that."

He doesn't mean anything by it; he is simply unaware this style of communication is off-putting and typically perceived as aggressive and rude. If he was aware of the impact his communication has on others, he might be amenable to change. He isn't aware, though. No matter how many times my team and I try to talk to him, he still doesn't understand. Yet, he still wonders why no one understands him.

If you don't understand others, how can you expect them to

understand you? We can all learn from Stephen Covey in the *7 Habits of Highly Effective People*. Habit 5 is "Seek first to understand, and then be understood."

One time in particular, this employee used this style to write an email to a client. They were convinced they didn't have everything they needed to get started on a project, so they drafted up a note with short bursts of facts and readied it for transmission.

Luckily, however, my executive team caught the email before it went out. Not only was the email worded in a way that may be offensive to the client, but it was also incorrect—the information this employee thought they were missing had been mislabeled as something else. If he had been more aware and open, he may have been slower to respond and recognize the labeling mishap. Instead, he responded with his ego. He cared so much about being right that he was completely unaware he was wrong. Your ego is not your amigo.

HOW TO BROADEN AWARENESS

Without awareness, we're in a constant state of uninformed optimism. We hope and pray we'll be able to resolve our problems, but if we're unaware of our insecurities—or the real cyberthreats facing our environment, for that matter—and how they play out daily at work, our ability to fix them is nonexistent. In order to solve problems, we need to first be aware of them. Awareness means recognizing our blind spots in order to fix them.

What we need instead is informed realism. We need to be fully aware of the truth of what is happening around us so we can make well-educated decisions to solve problems. The truth is often a hard pill to swallow. People generally have no problem with the truth about others, but when it comes to the truth about themselves, it is avoided.

How do we get there? How do we get our technical team to broaden their awareness and reach a state of informed realism?

COACHING

Many technical people lack awareness, and we need to encourage them to broaden it in order to grow. I believe one of the best methods to reach this objective is coaching.

Most of us look at our lives with blinders on—we only see what's directly in front of us. Working with a coach provides us with a bird's-eye view of our life and gives us insights we likely never would have discovered on our own. A coach has the ability to say, "I've heard you say you're doing *this* twelve times today, but you're actually doing *this*." A coach lives outside the box and can easily see your blind spots. You can also do this on your own. I like to "zoom out" of my life and look at it from above in a disassociated, objective state (like condor vision—more on this later). This helps me gather perspective.

There are many services out there that can help you coach your technical staff to reach a state of informed realism, but you probably picked up this book because you want to learn how to coach your team yourself.

I've coached my own team, and there are two main things you should focus on to broaden your technical team's awareness: perspective and state of mind.

Perspective

First, your technical people need to gain some perspective. We've talked about this already, but many of these employees are self-centered and think the world revolves around them or should. They haven't taken the time to put themselves in the shoes of the other person, so they jump to conclusions and get angry.

I'm generalizing, of course, but we've all seen it happen. Anyone who has worked with a technical person (or two, or ten, or ten thousand—you get the point) has seen this scenario play out again and again, all because the technical person couldn't see things from the other person's perspective or point of view.

This is due to a lack of awareness. If we're aware of other people's misfortunes and the things we have in common, we're more likely to be patient and understanding. If we put ourselves in the shoes of others, we will be more aware and will thus curb our behavior accordingly. As humans, we have the human condition in common, yet we typically overlook this and focus on superficial differences.

There are a few questions you can ask your employees when coaching them on perspective. You want to tell them to put themselves in the other person's shoes, but you want to say it differently.

Instead of this...*Can you put yourself in the other person's shoes?*

Ask this...*If X were in* your *shoes, what would that look like?*

This is a simple change, but it really flips the script. When you ask your technical employees to think about someone *else* relating to them first (versus the other way around), they naturally open up and think about the world from the other person's perspective.

You can use this tactic to coach your technical staff on how to better interact with their managers, too.

Instead of this...*How can you be more aware with what's happening on your team?*

Ask this...*How would you talk to your manager about being more aware with what's happening on your team?*

We, as leaders, have to be aware that our technical staff has a lack of awareness. This means being aware of the word choices we use. It's not easy to get your technical staff to lead with their hearts and see the world from other people's perspectives. But if we're aware of this and the type of communication that works best for these employee types, we can frame our communication to be more effective and impactful.

STOICISM

Stoicism is about managing your state and is a demonstration of evolvement. It means not taking things personally and not reacting emotionally or egotistically to external events and things that cannot be controlled. With Stoicism, the path to happiness is found by accepting the moment as it presents itself—by not being allowed to be controlled by a desire for pleasure or the avoidance of pain but rather by using your mind to understand the world and to do your part by working together and treating others fairly and justly.

People at Alpine Security and others I know practice Stoicism, and it has made a big difference in how they "show up." They are more centered, are less explosive (emotional), and bring a smaller amount of ego to the conversation. People who practice Stoicism have the patience to deal with the world and people as they are.[23] There is a quick TED-Ed video on Stoicism that is a great reference.[24]

State of Mind

It's also key to coach your technical staff on how to recognize, control, and direct their state of mind, because it's necessary to maintain the right one. Your state of mind has the power to impact the outcome of the situation and relationships you're in, which makes awareness of our state of mind critical to all our interactions with others.

If I'm in a confrontational state of mind and I don't recognize it, I'm likely to come off as such in the next meeting I'm invited to. If that happens, the meeting will likely be a bust, and my relationships with my colleagues will sour (no one likes their time wasted). All because of my state of mind.

DOUG COMPLETELY LOST IT

I'm a believer in managing your state—I think it's a sign of evolvement. Doug was unable to manage his state. He was extremely volatile, and he justified it by saying, "Well, at least you always know what I'm thinking and where I stand."

One day in a company meeting via Zoom, we were discussing some

23 Ryan Holiday, *The Obstacle Is the Way: The Timeless Art of Turning Trials into Triumph* (New York: Portfolio, 2014).

24 Massimo Pigliucci, "The Philosophy of Stoicism," TED-Ed, June 19, 2017, https://www.youtube.com/watch?v=R9OCA6UFE-0.

changes with our organizational structure, when I saw him get physically upset—he lashed out at the computer screen like he was trying to swat it. Then he completely lost it and closed his laptop lid fiercely.

This was just another sign I ignored because I was too focused on my heart. If I had listened to my head and my body, this would have been the final straw.

State of mind affects our decisions, too. We'll get into this more in the next chapter, but we make better decisions when we are in a **powerful state** (a state of abundance) rather than a **primal state** (a state of fear and scarcity). The trick is to get yourself in the right mental state before making big decisions (this plays into the next step in the methodology, mindset), which isn't always easy and takes a lot of practice. Think about the decisions you made in the past, what state of mind were you in when you made your best decisions? What state of mind were you in when you made your worst decisions?

Your technical people need to be aware of the effect and the power their state of mind can have on the business, their employees, and their clients.

COMMUNICATION

Coach your technical people on how to gain perspective. Coach them on how to maintain a positive state of mind, too. When you do, however, make sure you communicate your message effectively. If your technical people don't comprehend what you're coaching them to do, they won't be able to get to a place of informed realism—they won't be able to broaden their awareness.

Earlier, I said questions are powerful—ask a better question, get a better answer. One of the many things you learn as a coach is how to ask better questions. Our brain is wired to answer questions, and if you ask limiting questions, it will come up with weak, lame answers. If you ask your brain powerful questions, it will come up with dynamic, badass answers.

Communication, especially with technical people, needs to be very specific and very prescriptive. Don't assume they know anything. Don't assume they know terms such as *gross profit margin* or *revenue*. This is just "manager speak" to them. They have no idea what you're talking about and they don't care to know—just like they think *you* don't care to know and appreciate their world. When you talk to them using words they don't understand and about things they know nothing about, they'll look at you with a blank, disengaged stare.

And they won't tell you they don't understand the words you're using. They won't tell you they have no idea what you're talking about, and there will be communication breakdowns and security breaches as a result. Cybercriminals win because your technical staff didn't tell you they didn't understand what you were talking about. This is something we, as leaders, need to be aware of. This can be as simple as how you define a critical asset or your risk tolerance.

Make It Specific and Relatable

Do you remember the story about Karen earlier in the chapter?

I was so shocked that she asked for a raise (after I had explained to everyone that we were behind in revenue) that I sat back and thought, *Did my words fall on deaf ears? How could I have communicated our financial deficit more clearly?*

And it hit me. I wasn't being specific enough for my technical team to really grasp the reality of the situation. Karen was living in a world of uninformed optimism, and my words had failed to bring her over to my side of the fence.

If Karen was confused and unaware, how many others were, too?

So I decided to try a different tactic for next week's meeting and get more specific.

The following Monday, I sat with my team again to go over numbers. They had improved, but we still needed to dig in our heels to make our revenue targets. Instead of using high-level numbers, I broke it down into billable hours. I wanted to be very specific and get into the nitty-gritty.

Target Hourly Rate

Costs		
		$150
Sales Commission/Referral Fees	18%	$(27)
Blended Direct Employee Rate (Hourly)		$48
Direct Employee Overhead (Benefits, Taxes, etc.)	18%	$(57)
Blended Overhead Employee Rate (Hourly)	$25	
Overhead Employee Overhead (Benefits, Taxes, etc.)	18%	$(30)
Overhead (Lease, Software Licenses, Books, Materials, Contractors, etc.)	11%	$(17)
Bench Time, Study, Internal Training	8%	$(12)
		$(142)
Profit	5%	$8

Sample Project

	Revenue	Hours (WBS)		
	$10,000	67		

Use Case	Hours Worked	Total Cost	Profit for Hours Worked	Profit for Hours over/under Budget	Total Profit	%
1	62	$9,300	$496	$750	$1,246	12%
2	67	$10,050	$536	$0	$536	5%
3	72	$10,800	$536	$(800)	$(264)	-3%
4	77	$11,550	$536	$(1,550)	$(1,014)	-10%

Sample spreadsheet showing hourly breakdown and profit/loss projections, per fixed-price project, based on hours worked.

"We all know our target bill rate is $150 per hour, right?"

People nodded their heads around the room.

"Okay, good. And these are all our operating costs, per hour, broken out by percentage."

I pulled up a list of all our business costs. It included commissions, referral fees, salaries and benefits, software costs, the lease, and miscellaneous overhead.

"This is our profit per hour."

I showed them the profit line (I had a spreadsheet up on the conference room screen) and watched out of the corner of my eye as a few jaws dropped. After all the business costs, the profit per hour for an average project was *eight dollars*.

I then went on to explain that the profit margin of eight dollars was only good if the sample project was completed within the 67 hours. If it was, the company would profit $536, but if the project went over, even by five hours, profit would not only vanish, but the company would also be in the hole.

Next, I pulled up an image of a piggy bank.

"Every month the company is in the hole, we need to dip into the company piggy bank to cover the difference. The more we dip into it, the less money we have for raises and software and equipment upgrades. I wanted to show you all this so you know exactly how the money comes in and out of the organization. Any questions?"

After the meeting, Karen pulled me aside again. She said, "Now that I understand how it all works, if there is enough money for raises, I don't think I should be the first one to get one. I think there are other people here, like some of the other engineers maybe, who deserve it more."

I was shocked—it was a complete one-eighty. I was hoping my new strategy would work, but I wasn't expecting it to work that well. I've had some time to process the experience, and I think it all comes down to relatability. When the numbers are too high level, your technical staff can't relate. If you break it down more specifically, it suddenly becomes applicable and tangible. This specificity and relatability shows them exactly how they can influence the bottom line to help the company and get a raise.

Understand Their Motivation

You want to communicate effectively with your technical staff so you can help them broaden their awareness. To do that, you also need to understand what motivates them. When you do, you will be able to craft communication that not only lands but also sticks. The point of all this is to improve people skills and influence permanent change.

"TEFLON HEAD"

Many years ago, I used to work with a guy I referred to as Teflon Head. In meetings, he would ask questions in an attempt to collaborate, but in the end he only listened to and approved of his own ideas. He wasn't collaborative at all—nothing would stick. We even tried making our ideas seem like his, but that didn't work either. The only thing that stuck to this guy was his nickname.

Motivation is tricky, because it's different for everyone. Some of your staff may be motivated by money (stay away from these people if you can), and others may be motivated by altruism. Whatever the motivation, you need to find it if you want to be able to communicate effectively.

Territory Maps

Remember the NLP presuppositions I introduced in the previous chapter? **Territory maps** are an NLP concept and tie into the presuppositions that state there is no objective reality—that we each have an individual, unique map of the world (territory). We all have our own, unique territory maps.

Our territory map is how we interpret the world around us. It is our image of reality and causes us to we act and think the way we do. The words we speak and the way we communicate are not the same as the event or object they represent because they are influenced by our territory map.

Have you heard of the sayings, "Looking at the world through a different lens" or "One man's trash is another one's treasure"? Territory maps are like that. Everyone sees things differently (remember how we've talked about perspective previously). For example, where someone sees a problem, I almost always see an opportunity.

NLP dictates how you communicate with yourself and interact with your unique map. It's also how you communicate with *others* and interact with *their* unique maps and models of reality. (To remind you, this is just the tip of the NLP iceberg. Throughout the book, I will touch on NLP key concepts where relevant, but NLP is a very in-depth subject and deserves to be explored fully in a book of its own.)

A territory map is a good tool for us to use as coaches because it can help us discover our employees' individual motivations. If we understand how our employees view the world, we're more likely to know what excites them and makes them happy.

TIPS AND TRICKS: CONDOR VISION

Condor vision is a concept that asks us to zoom out and look at our lives from the perspective of a condor. When we do, we can see the entire terrain, where we are in it, what surrounds us, where we need to go, and more. It gives us perspective.

My coach practices shamanism and first told me about condor vision. According to Andean shamanic traditions, the condor represents our ability to rise above the concerns of daily life—the unnecessary dramas, anxieties, fears, doubts, and insecurities that often characterize modern living—and gain a transcendent perspective on what is truly most important.

Condor vision allows us to determine what is most significant to the evolution of our soul so we know what to focus on. This focus allows us to embrace a purposeful, loving, and spiritually aligned life path.

INFORMED REALISM

We all have blind spots. We all suffer from moments of uninformed optimism. My buddy was blinded to his problem with SimCity, and I was blinded by my need to be the smartest person in the room.

We are all capable of change, though. When my friend became aware that he was neglecting his real-life responsibilities, he quit the game. Awareness and informed realism were his catalyst for change.

Developing the people skills of our technical employees is tough, but it isn't impossible. If we can first broaden their awareness and open their eyes, we are one step closer to encouraging them to embrace change.

Awareness is one thing. Having the right mindset in order to commit to change is another. Next, let's talk about the second in the Secure Methodology—Mindset.

EXERCISE: BROADEN AWARENESS

In addition to the guidance on coaching I gave you earlier in the chapter, here are two activities you can do with your technical staff to help broaden their awareness.

Activity 1:
Understanding and Applying Context

Overview: Context can often be observed, yet the unseen context of what may be going on behind the scenes is typically just as important, if not more.

Objective: To understand how context affects your behavior and the behavior of others.

Preparation: No prep is needed for this activity.

Materials: Pen and paper.

Step 1: Read the following passage to your team (or give it to them in writing—it doesn't matter):

You have an important meeting downtown with your boss and you're running a little behind. When you get to your local coffee shop, you're shocked to see a line out the door. Normally, you would just grab coffee at the office, but there isn't going to be any at the meeting space downtown. So you have no choice but to wait—you really want the coffee.

When you get inside, you can see the cashier is new (you don't recognize her). You can also see she's taking forever to ring up each customer. It's starting to drive you crazy.

Step 2: Ask them the following question:

If you had the opportunity to complain about the cashier to the store manager, would you?

Step 3: When they're done answering, move on to the second of the activity, and read the following:

While waiting in line, you witness several customers yell at and berate the cashier. You think you see the cashier start to cry. Then you overhear the cashier tell one of the angry customers they just found out their grandmother is in the hospital.

Step 4: Ask them the following question:

Now knowing this, if you had the opportunity to complain about the cashier to the store manager, would you?

The struggles and challenges people often deal with are not typically apparent. You don't know what's going on with the cashier, and she doesn't know you're late for work.

What you're doing is giving your technical employee context. You're making them aware that other people have struggles and challenges, too.

Activity 2:
Reflect on the Previous Day

If you don't like that one, here's another you could try.

Overview: Growth comes from making time to pause, untangle, and sort through observations and experiences, consider multiple possible interpretations, create meaning, and determine ways to improve.

Objective: To understand how your state of mind affects your day-to-day activities and to reflect and learn what worked, what didn't work, and how to improve.

Preparation: No prep is needed for this activity.

Materials: Pen and paper.

Step 1: Have your technical employees think about the previous day.

Step 2: Ask them to jot down moments throughout the day where they were in a negative state of mind.

Step 3: Ask them to pick one moment, then drill down by asking the following questions:

- Why did that irritate you?

- What were you expecting?
- How did you communicate?
- How was your communication received?
- What are you going to do next time to prevent this?

Treat others like you would like to be treated. What if your interaction was the last one of your life? Not to be dramatic, but we never know what's going to happen in the future. We think we live a life of certainty, but we don't. So show a little compassion and kindness, and don't make assumptions.

Either activity should help broaden the awareness of your technical staff.

CHAPTER 4

▧ ▧ ▧

STEP 2: MINDSET

Whatever the mind can conceive and believe, it can achieve.

—NAPOLEON HILL

The 1999 science fiction film *The Matrix*, starring Keanu Reeves, Laurence Fishburne, and Carrie-Anne Moss, is one of my favorite films. It's about a time when machines rule the earth and man's journey (well, one man, Neo, in particular) to stop them.

One of my favorite scenes happens in the beginning of the movie when Neo (Reeves) has to choose between taking either a red pill or a blue pill. If he chooses the red pill, he will wake up in the matrix and see the truth. If he chooses the blue pill, he will go back to the life he once knew as if nothing ever happened.

Neo chooses the red pill, and the film's main adventure begins.

NLP PRESUPPOSITIONS FOR MINDSET

- **You are in charge of your mind and therefore your results.**
  (I am also in charge of my mind and therefore my results.)
- **People have all the resources they need to succeed and to achieve their desired outcomes.**
  (There are no unresourceful people, only unresourceful states.)
- **There is ONLY feedback!**
  (There is no failure, only feedback.)
- **The law of requisite variety.**
  (The system/person with the most flexibility of behavior will control the system.)
- **All procedures should be designed to increase choice.**

FIXED VERSUS GROWTH MINDSET

Having the right mindset is important in everything we do. In *The Matrix*, Neo has a choice to make, and the choice is a reference to his mindset. Does he want to take the red pill and see the truth? Or does he want to take the blue pill and ignore it?

In her book *Mindset: The New Psychology of Success*, Carol Dweck suggests mindset breaks down into two different categories. The first is **growth mindset**, and it means you are in charge of your own life. In NLP terminology, this concept means you are on the cause side of the equation, not the effect—that *you* cause everything around you, not the other way around. We represent this as Cause is greater than Effect (C > E). If you're on the effect side, the equation is E > C. In *The Matrix*, the red pill represents informed realism and a growth mindset.

Individuals with a growth mindset believe they can overcome challenging circumstances. They believe their brain is malleable—anything is possible if they set their mind to it. You'll often hear phrases such as "I can learn this," "It won't be easy, but I can do it," and "If I try, I can" come from people with a growth mindset because these individuals know how to come up with solutions in the direst of circumstances. In order to solve problems, they know how to have the courage to try something new.

People with a **fixed mindset**, on the other hand, don't think they're in charge of their own life. They think everything is set in stone, even themselves. They think they are on the effect side of the equation and their life is the *result* of everything around them. These individuals are close-minded and aren't open to new ideas.

"I'm just not that good at that." "I'm too old." "I'm not naturally gifted." "I can't learn that." You'll hear these phrases come from the mouths of fixed-mindset people. They have a limiting belief pattern because they see things in black or white. It's this way or that. It's all or nothing. You get the drift. People with a fixed mindset prefer a state of uninformed optimism and always take the blue pill.

RED PILL FUNCTIONALITY

I used to reverse engineer malicious software (malware) to determine its behavior, how to stop it, who wrote it, and so forth. In the old days (around 2010), when you reverse engineered malware, you ran the program in a virtual machine, often isolated from the internet. Malware authors knew this was the process, so they added **red pill functionality** to the malware, which cause it to behave differently when it was in a virtual environment. Because the malware operated differently, the cybersecurity engineer's job to reverse engineer the malware was more difficult. Red pill functionality gave malware a growth mindset.

TAKE OWNERSHIP OF YOUR ACTIONS

Having a growth mindset means taking ownership of your actions in order to learn from them. Otherwise you won't change, because it will always be someone else's fault.

Many people don't want to know the truth. That's why a lot of them avoid going to the doctor—they want to sidestep difficult conversations. It takes courage to have ownership and face the truth. With cybersecurity, the only way to change is to start from a place of honesty. If we aren't honest about the status of the security—if we pretend things are okay, or we have it "all covered" when we don't—we're asking for trouble.

People with growth mindsets take responsibility for their own lives and the effect they have on others. They're aware and willing to change. They take the red pill. To have a fixed mindset means just the opposite. It means you're so unwilling to change that you would rather turn a blind eye to the truth. You'd rather stay in your own unhappiness than risk the unknown, which could be better. People with a fixed mindset choose the blue pill. They choose to stay in the matrix and continue to run the hamster wheel of life, even though they know it's pointless.

FIXED MINDSET AND GROWTH MINDSET

FIXED MINDSET

"Failure is the limit of my abilities"

"I don't like to be challenged"

"I'm either good at it or I'm not. I can either do it or not"

"Feedback and criticism are personal"

"My potential is predetermined"

"When I'm frustrated, I give up"

"I shy away from uncertainty and stick to what I know"

GROWTH MINDSET

"Failure is an opportunity to learn"

"challenges help me grow"

"My effort and attitude determine my abilities"

"Feedback is necessary and constructive"

"I can learn to do anything I want"

"I'm inspired by the success of others"

"I embrace uncertainty and try new things"

Fixed versus growth mindset.

THE IMPACT ON CYBERSECURITY

Neo chooses the red pill because he has a growth mindset. He wants to know the truth and he's open to change. If you've seen the movie, you know the changes Neo went through were uncomfortable and difficult. So much so that one of the characters who took the red pill wanted to go back into the matrix in order to avoid the truth. In cybersecurity, we need to take the red pill and face the truth.

Having a growth mindset in cybersecurity is paramount because an open mind is a mind that's amenable to change. If your technical employees aren't open-minded, they're content sticking with one-hundred-question checklists and other overly complicated solutions that are outrageously expensive and don't always work. People without a growth mindset can't wrap their head around anything new, including solutions that may require a different way of looking at problems.

We worked with a company a few years back that had medical devices in hospitals and clinics all over the world. Their devices were all password protected—if a service tech needed access to a device, they had to get the password.

My team was brought on to test for vulnerabilities, and we found one. We discovered that the company's simple password-generating algorithm had been leaked on the internet. Every password to every device was completely accessible.

You can imagine how freaked out the company was when we told them. We told them the original intent of the leak wasn't malicious—a few of the techs thought it would be helpful if all the techs had access to the passwords—but it didn't matter. The damage had been done.

A day later, the CISO presented a very complicated authentication system that required major technical components and would cost the company roughly one million dollars. We suggested something much simpler (and cost effective), but the CISO fought it tooth and nail. He was dead set on his method, and nothing was going to change his mind.

He had a fixed mindset. He wasn't open to new ideas because he let his ego get in the way. He had to be the smartest person in the room. If he had been, he would have saved his company a lot of time and a lot of money—money that could have been spent on other cybersecurity initiatives to fortify their offering. Instead, he wanted to do it his way, no matter what. We're losing the war because of people like that: they're too close-minded to change.

When you have the right mindset, you look at the glass as half-full rather than half-empty. You commit to the industry (for the right reasons) and are open to change. We must take ownership of the cybersecurity war and why we are losing.

Neo chose the red pill because he was open to change. You want your technical team (especially your technical leadership) to reach for the red pill, too.

HIRED TO BREAK IN

In 2013, I did a penetration test for a bank in California. There are a few different types of penetration tests. There are technical penetration tests that focus around computers and hacking, physical tests, like picking locks, and social engineering tests that center on human interaction. There are also penetration tests that are a combination of all three. Regardless of the test, the general purpose is the same—to break in and steal valuable information. For this particular gig, I was tasked with a social engineering penetration test. My objective was to get into a specific bank branch and steal files.

I didn't have a lot of time to prepare, so I pretended to be a new hire for the bank but for a different branch.

I approached the bank I was tasked to penetrate before it was open to the public. I rang the bell for service, and a woman (Sally, the branch administrator) answered the door. Sally eyed me wearily.

"Hi, I'm a new hire at the branch on the other side of town. Bob [the general manager] asked me to stop by today to pick up in-processing paperwork. He wants me to hit the ground running."

Sally was reluctant to let me in, but I gave her the general manager's name (it was easy to look that information up on the internet) and looked official (I was in a suit), so she did. She then escorted me back to her desk and asked me to take a seat.

"I'm going to call Bob and figure out exactly what you need. Give me a few minutes," Sally said as she left her office to call Bob. While she was gone, I spied three files sitting on her desk. I grabbed them and slipped them into my briefcase.

"I wasn't able to get a hold of Bob," she said when she came back into the office a few minutes later. (I knew she wouldn't because I had done my research—Bob wasn't in the branch this early in the morning.) "I don't know what paperwork to give you, so you'll have to come back later. I'm sorry."

I told her I understood as I stood to leave.

"Thanks anyway for your help," I said as I turned and walked back out of the bank.

Later that morning, I met with my client point of contact, Jessica, who wasn't very pleased to see the three files I stole from Sally's desk. Jessica asked me to head back to the bank to debrief the team on the results of the penetration test.

When Sally found out what I had done, she started to cry. She never even noticed the files were missing. She broke three bank rules that morning—she let me, a nonbranch employee, in the bank before hours, she left sensitive company data on her desk, and she left me (a stranger) unattended.

I mention this example because I often think about what happened to Sally. Was she fired for breaking the rules?

My mindset around the situation is different than that. Yes, she broke the rules, but she'll never break them again. She learned the hard way what can happen if you aren't hyperdiligent about data security, so I would think she would be *extra* cautious. Her direct experience with a data breach makes her an asset.

COMMITMENT

In order to win the cybersecurity war (and defeat the invisible thieves trying to steal your data), your technical staff needs to have a growth mindset. They also need to commit to it. What good is having a growth mindset if you aren't actually committed to making the change? Without a growth mindset, it's nearly impossible to commit to the challenge of trying something new in order to solve a difficult problem. It's easy to have a fixed mindset and rely on solutions that have worked in the past, but it's hard to go against the grain and do something different and possibly face criticism. (That's okay, though—unlike activists and people who matter, there are no statues of critics.) Having a growth mindset is good, but without the commitment to change, it's practically useless.

What's more, if you aren't committed to cybersecurity, you're probably not going to be committed to fighting cybercrime and winning the war. And if you aren't committed to winning the war, you're probably not going to do a good job of protecting data.

You need to make sure your technical people are committed for the right reasons, too. We talked about this in the beginning of the book—a lot of people are in cybersecurity for the money. They know they can make a lot of money in this industry, so they get the certification (or the degree) and they obtain a job securing data simply to stuff their wallets full of cash.

However, it has been my experience that these types of individuals ultimately fail. Cybersecurity is a tough industry. The pressure is intense because people's lives (and livelihoods) are at stake and budgets are often nearly nonexistent. The industry moves fast and is always struggling for enough resources. To survive and defend against cybercriminals, you have to be nimble, creative, and willing to go the extra mile to ensure the work gets done correctly. If you aren't passionate about protecting data, it's easy to get overwhelmed and then swept away. When you have the right mindset, you're in it for the right reasons—you're not just in it for the money.

IS COMMITMENT DIFFERENT THAN MINDSET?

Is there a difference between *mindset* and *commitment*? Absolutely.

Mindset is how you view the objective or the problem. It's glass half-empty (fixed) or glass half-full (growth). Commitment is completing the steps needed to complete the objective or solve the problem, no matter how difficult. A growth mindset implies commitment because it's how you learn.

Thomas Edison's teachers said he was "too stupid to learn anything." He was even fired from his first couple of jobs for being a slacker. Edison had a growth mindset, though. As an inventor, Edison made nearly one thousand unsuccessful attempts before *successfully* inventing the light bulb. It was an invention with one thousand steps. Edison demonstrated a growth mindset and a commitment, and he embraced the NLP presupposition, "There is ONLY feedback! (There is no failure, only feedback.)"

We talked about this a little already, but what good is a growth mindset if you are unwilling to take the steps necessary to evolve? If you aren't committed, you can't change. Without action, who cares what your mindset is?

Mindset and commitment are related, but commitment is the evolution. Mindset is being open to that evolution, but commitment is the action required to get there.

NEO, THE DOBERMAN

I used to have a Doberman I named Neo. Even though the dog was female, we (my ex-wife and I) named her Neo. At the time, I really embraced what *The Matrix* stood for (a growth mindset versus a fixed one). I liked the reminder every time I called her by her name.

A COMMITMENT TO CYBERSECURITY

When you have a growth mindset and are committed to defeating cybercriminals, it's easier to feel connected to your work and thus do a great job. If you're pursuing a career in cybersecurity for the right reasons, you will feel connected to the industry on a deeper level.

I have referenced the "right reasons" several times now, but I haven't fully explained those reasons. Pursuing a career in cybersecurity for the right reasons means you're in it for the greater good. You want to fight cybercriminals because you want to help make the world a better place, make sure hackers don't attack your grandmother via medical devices, and prevent fraud. You are passionate about protecting sensitive information, and you want to fight the bad guys.

I'm committed to cybersecurity because I want to effect change in a positive manner. I want to have an impact and help amplify the positive impact others make. Specifically, I don't want to see small and medium businesses (SMBs) suffer at the hands of nefarious black hat hackers and get stuck paying for a credit monitoring service (for each client record stolen) for multiple years. These credit monitoring fees will probably cause the SMB to go bankrupt. I know how hard it is to build a small business, and I am passionate about protecting them.

I'm also passionate about protecting healthcare and medical devices from being weaponized. I don't want to see people being held hostage to ransomware because their life depends on it. I don't want to see medical devices used for terrorism (like we talked about at the beginning of the book), and I don't want to see people die. I want to protect a child's lifesaving medical device from being hacked, and I want to prevent someone from being threatened by ransomware. I pursue a career in cybersecurity because someone I love could be hurt or injured, and I want to do everything I can to stop it.

I'm not saying your technical team should be pursuing a career in cybersecurity for the same reasons I am, but I *am* saying they should be pursuing it for something other than money or status. They shouldn't be pursuing cybersecurity because it sounds cool. They should be pursuing it because they feel passionate about it. Without that passion, a growth mindset and commitment and connection to the work, real improvement to the industry simply won't happen. The "clock in, clock out" mindset does not cut it for a professional career in cybersecurity.

TIPS AND TRICKS: HOW TO DEVELOP
A GROWTH MINDSET

A successful professional career in cybersecurity requires a growth mindset. To help your technical team develop one, there are a few things you, as a coach, can do.

First, you can start by encouraging reflection. Reflection is a great mindset tool because it allows us to think about how we would do things differently. Thinking about alternative solutions is a sign of growth.

You can ask the right questions, too. (I mentioned this concept earlier.) For people who are stuck, I often ask, "What are *two* things you could do to improve this situation?" I ask for two things (as opposed to one) because it naturally expands their thinking.

I also like to ask, "If you needed to improve ten times by X date, what are a few things you would do differently? What would you start doing, what would you stop doing, and what would you continue to do?" These questions get them to think differently and help them grow and change.

Finally, I encourage quick decision making. In my own life, I place everything into either a "Hell Yes" or a "Hell No" bucket. "Maybe" lives on the effect side of the cause-and-effect equation and is the enemy of ownership. A maybe mindset is a mindset based on fear. I move items out of the "Maybe" bucket as quickly as possible.

When coaching, there is one thing to remember. Coaching, unlike therapy, is designed to move life forward. Coaches don't spend a lot of time trying to resolve past traumas—we work to first create a compelling image of the future and then determine how best to get there.

We all have the answers inside ourselves. A coach is the person who helps you uncover/reveal them. We already know what to do; we just need to get rid of the garbage that's in the way. The best coaches don't give advice—they help you discover the best way to help yourself.

THE POWER OF WHY

In the last chapter, we said you can communicate more effectively when you know your employees' motivations. Motivation is tied to mindset, too—what motivates your employees to commit to cybersecurity? Without the right motivation, it's hard to have the right mindset and the commitment to accomplish our goals and stop cybercriminals. It's also impossible to form a new habit. (Motivation is great to get you to start something new, but a habit is what keeps it going.) Let me give you an example.

Jonas is in his early sixties and struggles with his health and specifically his weight. He wants to shed some weight (and has for years) but can never seem to get himself to the gym consistently for more than two weeks at a time. Plus, his eating habits are atrocious. He doesn't even bother dieting anymore because he ends up throwing his new health food away on day two. Jonas wants to lose weight but can't get motivated to actually *do* it.

Many of us struggle with staying motivated. For years, we tell people we want to lose weight or quit smoking or get a new job, yet we continue to sit back and do nothing to realize our goals. We don't take the steps necessary to actually do what we say we're going to do because we haven't tapped into what truly motivates us, our why.

True motivation (the kind that leads to forming new habits and seeing real change) lies deep beneath the surface. The best way to access it is to drill down until you strike oil and find it. Called the 7 Levels Deep Exercise,[25] this can be achieved by asking, "Why?" (It takes the average person seven questions, hence the title, but it may take you or your team six or nine. It's important to note everyone's results will be different.) I first heard of this exercise from Dean Graziosi in his book *Millionaire Success Habits*, which I listened to on audible, typically while hiking or working out.

When Jonas was asked why he wanted to lose the weight, he said, "I want to feel healthier."

He was then asked, "Why do you want to feel healthier?"

"Well, I want to have more vitality."

"Why?"

Jonas scratched his chin. "I want to be able to walk up and down the stairs without breathing heavily."

"Why do you want to do that?"

"I want to age well," he said quickly.

"Why is aging well important to you?"

At this, Jonas paused for a moment and then said, "I want to be able to play with my grandkids."

"Why do you want to play with them?"

---

25 "7 Levels of Deep: Discover Your Why," accessed November 13, 2020, http://www.7levelsdeep. com/.

"When I was a kid, all I wanted to do was play with my grandfather, but he died before I ever had a chance."

Once the onion's layers were peeled back, Jonas's true motivation/purpose for getting healthy was exposed. He wanted to be there for his grandchildren because his grandfather wasn't there for him. As soon as Jonas's true purpose for losing weight was revealed, he had no problem losing the weight. He had found his reason why.

Keep in mind that to do this exercise correctly, you must be emotionally connected to the why. Each level of questioning should feel more visceral and more emotional than the last. Otherwise, you're still leading with your head. For an example, check out Lewis Howes's video interview with Dean Graziosi.[26]

Everyone needs a reason to do something. Some people pursue cybersecurity for the money and others because they want to stop cybercrime. To get your technical employees to commit to improving their people skills in order to grow (and form a new habit so they continue to grow), you have to first find out what motivates them.

---

26   Dean Graziosi, "7 Levels Deep: To Success," YouTube, September 12, 2018, https://www.youtube.com/watch?v=Sv882g7UVQE.

THE WHY LOOP

Sometimes the 7 Levels Deep Exercise can create a "why loop." Someone will say they want A, and when you ask them why, they'll tell you it's because they want B. When you ask them about B, they tell you they want B because they also want A.

When this happens, listen for keywords and what *isn't* being said. Then change your line of questioning. Instead of asking why questions, ask what and how questions, like we talked about in the beginning of the book.

CHOOSE THE RED PILL

Neo had a growth mindset. He was motivated to learn the truth, so he chose the red pill.

Do you know who *doesn't* have a growth mindset? Doug. He talks down to people, hops from job to job, and freaks out under pressure, but he thinks he's doing just fine. If you asked Doug what he thought he needed to fix about himself, he'd say, "Nothing." (He's the smartest person in the room, remember?) That's why Doug has a difficult time succeeding.

It's hard to achieve success with a fixed mindset. When your technical employees have a fixed mindset, they are more likely to offer up complicated solutions that don't always get the job done. They're also less likely to be committed to change and the cybersecurity industry overall.

Change is *hard*, and most people want to stay in their comfort zones, technical people especially. I would rather live on the edge, but most people want to stay as far away from it as possible. What they don't realize, though, is having a growth mindset means being committed to taking the *first step* toward the edge. It doesn't mean teetering on it.

If you're not living a life on the edge you're taking up too much space![27]

—JIM WHITTAKER, FIRST AMERICAN TO CLIMB MOUNT
EVEREST AND AUTHOR OF *A LIFE ON THE EDGE*

Without a growth mindset and can-do attitude, it's difficult to get our technical people out of their comfort zones to achieve success. In cybersecurity, our purpose is to prevent cyberattacks, but we're losing the war (many of us are losing the internal war, too). That means the tactics and frameworks we're comfortable and familiar with aren't working.

We have to change these tactics and frameworks even though it will probably be uncomfortable. Progress doesn't happen by being comfortable and following the status quo. It's easy to fall into that trap and think things will change if we keep doing what we're doing—but things won't change unless we do.

Our technical employees need to be committed and feel connected to cybersecurity. They also need to be open to growth and change. Only then will we win the war.

Now that our technical employees are aware they lack people skills, have an open mindset, and are committed to change, it's time for some acknowledgment. Step three is coming up.

---

27 Jim Whittaker, *A Life on the Edge: Memoirs of Everest and Beyond* (Seattle: The Mountaineers, 1999).

EXERCISE: DEVELOP A GROWTH MINDSET

Having a growth mindset is key to individual success as well as the success of the cybersecurity industry. Here are two activities to help you and/or your team develop one.

Activity 1:
7 Levels Deep

Do you know what truly motivates your team? Understanding motivation is the key to inspiring change and establishing new habits. Without understanding someone's true motivation, growth and change is difficult. In this activity, you will ask visceral and emotional questions to peel back the layers and understand your team's true motivation.

Overview: Understanding your underlying drivers and why you do what you do helps improve your mindset and gives you the drive to push through obstacles that are in the way of your desires. Your why should be emotional, not "in your head."

Objective: To uncover your underlying reason for why you really want to do something.

Preparation: No preparation is needed for this activity.

Materials: Pen and paper.

Step 1: Start with asking your team member something simple, such as, "Why did you start working in the industry?"

Step 2: Listen thoughtfully to their response, then ask your next question.

Step 3: Repeat this until you get to the heart of your team member's reason for working in cybersecurity. This should be visceral and emotional.

As a reminder, you can ask as many (or as few) questions as you need. Seven is the average number of questions asked. For some, it could take as few as four or five questions, and for others, nine or ten. Everyone will be different.

The 7 Levels Deep Exercise is not about finding your purpose, although it may help. It's really about revealing your underlying reason for doing (or wanting to do) something.

Activity 2:
5-Minute Journal

Reflection and a growth mindset go hand in hand. In order to grow, we must reflect on our past and learn from it. In this exercise, you and your team will each keep a journal and write in it for five minutes a day. (This activity is highlighted in *The Five-Minute Journal*.[28]) You can do this for as little or as long as you'd like, but I recommend doing it for at least thirty days.

Overview: Starting and ending the day with positive intent and gratitude improves overall well-being and mindset. Improved well-being and mindset affect how you interact with others, which affects your success and fulfillment.

Objective: Improved gratitude, well-being, and mindset after thirty days of journaling.

Preparation: No prep is needed for this activity.

---

28   https://www.amazon.com/Five-Minute-Journal-Happier-Minutes/dp/0991846206

Materials: Notebooks for your team to use as journals, pens.

Step 1: Meet with your team to introduce them to the exercise.

Step 2: Pass out the notebooks.

Step 3: Tell your team the journal entry should include the following five prompts and questions:

First thing in the morning...

I am grateful for...

What would make today great?

Daily affirmations. I am...

Right before bed...

Three amazing things that happened today

How could I have made today even better?

Step 4: Remind your team daily to complete their journal entries by resending the list of prompts.

At the end of the journaling period, reconnect with your team. Ask them to reflect on the reflection exercise itself to see how much they've grown.

CHAPTER 5

※ ※ ※

STEP 3: ACKNOWLEDGMENT

Leaders don't look for recognition from others; leaders look for others to recognize.

—SIMON SINEK

David Goggins is an ultramarathon runner, an ultradistance cyclist, and triathlete. He's also a former Navy SEAL and motivational speaker. He's an author, too. His book, *Can't Hurt Me: Master Your Mind and Defy the Odds*, resonated with me, and I especially connect with his cookie jar concept. I listened to this book on audible.com, and it is easily one of the best books I've ever listened to, not only because of the content but also because it is delivered as a podcast with discussions between Adam Skolnick (narrator) and David Goggins.

Every time Goggins accomplishes something tough, he puts a virtual cookie of his accomplishment in a cookie jar.[29] He does this for every major accomplishment and demanding goal, and he does it for two reasons.

First, it's a tangible acknowledgment of his accomplishments.

---

29   David Goggins, "The Cookie Jar," YouTube, November 14, 2018, https://www.youtube.com/watch?v=5eO4DvOrf4Q.

(In order to acknowledge others, you first need to acknowledge yourself and your own accomplishments.) Each time he places a new "cookie" in the jar, he gives himself credit for achieving a milestone or overcoming an obstacle. It's a virtual pat on the back and encouragement to keep going.

Second, the cookie jar stores inspiration every time he is up against something especially tough. Anytime he feels like he can't continue, he reaches into the cookie jar and looks at the cookies in there to remind himself of everything he's already accomplished and how far he's already come. The cookie jar helps him get over the hump of self-doubt. If he accomplished something challenging before, he can do it again.

Goggins's cookie jar tactic stuck with me, so I started using it myself. Now, every time I accomplish something tough (like an Ironman triathlon or a big project), I acknowledge myself and put the cookies in my jar. It's an easy way for me to see how far I've come.

NLP PRESUPPOSITIONS FOR ACKNOWLEDGMENT

- **Everyone is doing the best they can with the resources they have available.**
  (Behavior is geared for adaptation, and present behavior is the best choice available. Every behavior is motivated by a positive intent.)
- **Behavior and change are to be evaluated in terms of context and ecology.**
- **People are not their behaviors.**
  (Accept the person; change the behavior.)
- **People have all the resources they need to succeed and to achieve their desired outcomes.**
  (There are no unresourceful people, only unresourceful states.)

EXPERT-LEVEL THINKING

Goggins's cookie jar represents the idea that if something tough was accomplished in the past, something tough can be accomplished again in the future. All we have to do is acknowledge it.

Acknowledgment is the expression of appreciation, and many executives and cybersecurity leaders don't know how to acknowledge the accomplishments of their technical staff. They misunderstand how difficult and how layered the cybersecurity industry is, so they misunderstand the skills of their cybersecurity team. Sometimes we get too caught up in the details or in the moment. Acknowledgment often requires us to zoom out of the moment and see how far we've come or what's gone "right" rather than "wrong." It's an easy trap to look through the lens of what went wrong instead of what went right. There will always be things that did not go right. Bigger problems typically equal progress. If you continually run into the same problem, this is not progress.

THE BIGGER THE GROWTH, THE BIGGER THE PROBLEMS

A lot of people have the idea that life should be problem-free. I disagree. If you are growing, you should have *bigger* problems than you had before. That's growth.

You already know the solution to the simpler and smaller problems. Growth requires solving the harder and larger ones. This is especially true for cybersecurity.

As humans, we typically want to find the easy way, but that's not how we grow. With cybersecurity, we need to grow and do things differently; otherwise, we'll continue to lose the cybersecurity war.

Acknowledgment and reward are more of a "carrot" versus a "stick" approach to leadership. A stick is more of an admonishment or punishment approach. Generally speaking, leading with a carrot—or attracting (pulling) your people toward great work—is better than pushing them.

"Pulling" forward with a carrot is better than "pushing" with a stick.

We often hear people say things like "**Cybersecurity** should be able to do that."

What these people don't understand is that cybersecurity is an entire industry, and there are many different specializations. There are experts in forensics, ethical hacking, and web application security. There are also experts in physical and wireless security. The list really does go on and on.

Company leaders often expect their technical employees to be experts in everything "technical," but can a doctor who specializes in oncology also specialize in optometry? Let's say this person is a Stephen Hawking type and really is smart enough to specialize in two unique but connected fields of medicine.

Do you think this person would also be able to specialize in two more, like podiatry and neurology? No doctor knows everything there is to know about every different medical field, so why should leadership expect their technical staff to know everything there is to know about cybersecurity?

Foundational knowledge in cybersecurity is tough enough—you often have to understand things such as IP address subnetting, how malware covertly propagates, what all the common ports and protocols are, and more. You may have to know differences between malware types, how to detect each type, and how to remove them. Finally, you need to understand cybersecurity risk and how cybersecurity relates to business.

In cybersecurity, knowledge builds on itself. No one can start at expert-level thinking. Many executives assume anyone in IT or cybersecurity can automatically start working at a high level on any relevant topic. For example, they think it's possible to be an expert in penetration testing today and a digital forensics expert tomorrow.

THE KSA MODEL

In cybersecurity, we need to focus on KSA: knowledge, skills, and abilities.

- **Knowledge** focuses on the understanding of concepts.
- **Skills** are the practical application of theoretical knowledge.
- **Abilities** are the innate traits or talents that a person brings to a task or situation.

Skills and abilities are often confused, yet there is a subtle and important difference. Abilities are typically achieved through experience.

Knowledge, skills, and abilities are all different, and we need people with all three. Paper tigers may have knowledge but no skills or abilities.

It takes loads of work and effort to become an expert in any one area of cybersecurity, just like it takes effort to become an expert in the medical field. You don't graduate high school and immediately earn your PhD—you have to earn your bachelor's and master's first. After that, you have to pick a specialty. You can't expect a neurosurgeon to understand how to fix your teeth. Cybersecurity is no different. For example, penetration testing is a niche area of cybersecurity with many different facets. There's wireless, database, network, web application, physical security, social engineering, mobile application, and more. Too many people throw the term *expert* around when it comes to cybersecurity because they don't know enough about it.

Executives and cybersecurity leadership often don't acknowledge how difficult cybersecurity is; that's why they expect everyone to be an expert. This is sort of like a business executive being an expert in everything business—marketing, sales, finance, operations, human resources, strategy, vision, tactics, mergers and acquisitions, and so forth. Don't get me wrong, cybersecurity is not complicated; it is actually simple, just not easy. The part that is typically missed is the simple part—people tend to overly complicate it due to the lack of understanding, posturing, and egos we've discussed so far.

A SYSTEMIC ISSUE

And that lack of acknowledgment trickles down. Company leaders don't acknowledge technical leaders for their hard work, and technical leaders don't acknowledge the employees on the front lines for *their* hard work. This issue is systemic. You often end up with a "kiss up, kick down" scenario, where the people on the "front lines" feel the brunt of attacks, both from cybercriminals (external) and from the kick-down managers (internal).

Technical leaders recognize how tough cybersecurity is, but they expect perfection. Instead of celebrating small wins, they criticize the one thing that was wrong. Everything else on the overcomplicated checklist could be impeccable, but if one thing was missed (or done incorrectly), all hell will break loose.

I'm exaggerating, of course, but that technical employee certainly won't be acknowledged for the good work they've done (even though the odds are stacked heavily against them). Instead, they'll be chastised for not getting it 100 percent right. This criticism is justified by management because that one wrong thing could lead to catastrophe—it could cause a data breach that exposes sensitive client data, resulting in negative financial and legal ramifications for the organization.

And to add salt to the wound, chances are, most technical people's families don't understand what they do and don't acknowledge them either. I've worked with several people who were never acknowledged at home for their work in cybersecurity because they "sat all day in front of a computer" instead of doing tangible things.

Because our technical leaders only acknowledge when things go wrong, it means they *don't* acknowledge when things go *right*. This lack of acknowledgment for the technical employees in the trenches causes problems because it has a negative impact on their work. It's hard to do your job, day in and day out, without any positive acknowledgment, especially in an industry like cybersecurity where everything is heightened and intense.

CHEAT SHEET: GIVE GOOD FEEDBACK

It's easy to give good feedback. Simply do the following:

1. Create a safe space. (Praise in public; provide constructive feedback in private.)
2. Be positive. (No one likes to only hear what they are doing wrong.)
3. Be specific and factual. (Generalities get missed.)
4. Be immediate. (The brain forgets if too much time passes.)
5. Be tough, not mean. (Ask for their perspective, acknowledge efforts, and correct behavior. Don't name call.)

THE SANDWICH APPROACH

Without acknowledgment, you can't build rapport. And without rapport, the opportunity for feedback is lost.

If you want to give your technical employee some constructive criticism, I suggest using what I call the **sandwich approach.** I didn't invent this, and I first heard of it in leadership training in the military.

The sandwich approach is a layered approach to employee feedback. The first layer is acknowledgment. Instead of hitting them with a criticism right off the bat, start with something they've done right. People are generally more receptive to feedback when they are not on the defensive. Stating something positive up front lets them know you appreciate them.

"That training deck you put together on ethical hacking was really well done. I especially like the demo you walked through. I know doing demos in live training can be challenging. Great job!"

Be as specific as you can with compliments—just saying "Good job," "You rock," and such like is not optimal. Appreciation through a compliment can make a technical employee feel good.

After the acknowledgment, the next layer in your sandwich is the constructive feedback.

"I want to talk to you about something else. That email you sent to your coworker was a little harsh. Is something going on?" Be as specific as possible, and make sure you discuss a plan with concrete steps on how to improve. The ideas for improvement should come from the person receiving the feedback.

Feedback should be timely and specific.

Because you started with an acknowledgment, your employee will be more receptive to feedback for improvement. As we've already talked about, an acknowledgment tells them you appreciate them and aren't just using them. They'll be more likely to trust you.

Don't end the conversation there, though. This isn't an open-faced sandwich. Close it off and end with something positive.

"I really have seen an improvement to your commitment to both your job and this company. Keep up the good work."

This way, you leave on a high note. You don't want your employee focusing on the negative. You want them to be aware of any challenges or issues so they make improvements (which means a plan and timeline for those improvements). But if you end the conversation positively, the results will be more long-lasting. Your employees will feel appreciated and respected.

THE BIGGEST COOKIE IN THE JAR

In its natural state, life is meaningless. (I believe so anyway.) We attach meaning to experiences, so we might as well attach something that serves us rather than hinders us.

A lot of us had a difficult childhood. My childhood—and the obstacles I overcame during it—is part of my cookie jar. It is probably the biggest cookie in the jar. If I could get through that, I should be able to get through just about anything. That cookie made me stronger.

The bottom line: if we attach the right meaning, we can learn from every experience, positive or negative. Rather than saying "That sucked" or "I'm such a failure," ask yourself, "What can I learn from that experience?"

THE IMPACT ON CYBERSECURITY

A lack of acknowledgment in cybersecurity has led to problems in the industry. It's one of the many reasons why we're losing the war. Without positive acknowledgment, our technical people become disengaged and forget all the good reasons why they joined this fight in the first place. This only reinforces stereotypes, which prevents them from learning anything new. A lack of acknowledgment even bleeds into the solutions our technical employees are presenting. Knowing all this, is it surprising that cybercriminals are winning?

RESENTFUL AND DISENGAGED

Technical people want to be acknowledged and appreciated for their hard work—they want credit for everything good they've done.

"Great job escalating privileges during the penetration test on Acme's web server, Yvonne. This will help us show them the true risk of the vulnerability they thought wasn't that big of a deal."

Isn't that true for all of us?

(Some of you might be thinking, *How am I supposed to know the details of a penetration test? I'm the CEO!* If we, as leaders, expect technical employees to communicate in a way that we can understand, we should also expect ourselves to understand and use more technical jargon so they can understand us.)

Most employees, regardless of industry, leave a company because they feel underappreciated. It's hardly ever about the money.[30] Without any appreciation or acknowledgment, employees become bitter, toxic, and disengaged. Thinking back on your career, have you ever worked with someone like that? I have worked with people so resentful that when they finally left, I felt a sense of relief.

Now think about technical employees and the work they're responsible for—securing your data or medical devices. If these types of employees are engaged, how do you think it will impact the quality of their work?

---

30 Marcel Schwantes, "Why Do People Quit Their Jobs, Exactly? It Comes Down to 3 Reasons, according to Research," *Inc.*, December 4, 2019, https://www.inc.com/marcel-schwantes/why-do-people-quit-their-jobs-exactly-it-comes-down-to-3-reasons-according-to-research.html.

Acknowledgment leads to engagement. You want to positively acknowledge your technical employees so they continue to do outstanding work. Every time they overcome something challenging, put a cookie in the cookie jar, remember it, and remind them.

THE 5 LANGUAGES OF APPRECIATION

Whether or not you are struggling to learn how to better appreciate your technical team, *The 5 Languages of Appreciation in the Workplace: Empowering Organizations by Encouraging People* by Gary Chapman and Paul White is an excellent resource.

The 5 Languages of Appreciation in the Workplace:

Words of Affirmation

Examples: Praise for accomplishments, affirmation of character, praise for personality

Quality Time

Examples: Engaging conversation, shared experiences, small-group dialogue, close proximity on a project

Acts of Service

Examples: Offer help, do it their way, complete what you start

Tangible Gifts

Examples: Time off, favorite food, concert tickets, gift card, bonus

Physical Touch

Examples: Handshakes, touching shoulders, brief hugs (especially during emotional times), high/low fives, fist bumps

TANGIBLE GIFTS	QUALITY TIME	WORDS OF AFFIRMATION	PHYSICAL TOUCH	ACTS OF SERVICE

Appreciation should be communicated based on the receiver's preferred language.

Most people gravitate toward two of the five. Knowing which ones your technical staff gravitate toward will help you acknowledge them more effectively.

INCORRECTLY FOCUSED

If we *do* acknowledge our technical employees but mention only their failures instead of their accomplishments (like our "kiss up, kick down" technical leaders tend to do), we run into a different set of problems—our technical employees start to emphasize the wrong things.

Instead of focusing on what they can do right, our technical employees focus on what they're doing wrong. Negative acknowledgment (the stick) forces them to think about their mistakes instead of their victories. Fear of making mistakes leads to inaction and complacency—the carrot is better than the stick. It's extremely difficult to visualize success when the emphasis is entirely on failure.

Let me give you an example. If you're at a public pool, and a big sign on the wall reads, "Don't slip on the floor!" all you're going to think about is slipping on the floor. And if you only think about slipping on the floor, chances are, you're going to slip.

If the sign reads, "Walk carefully!" you're going to think about walking carefully. You're going to move slowly and think about each step. And you know what? You're probably not going to slip.

When we acknowledge positive behavior, like walking carefully, the focus will be on that positive behavior. That is what we, as leaders, want.

REINFORCED STEREOTYPES

Focusing on what's wrong only reinforces stereotypes. It also creates a systemic, perpetual problem. "He's GREAT with computers, but he's terrible at talking to clients" or, "She sure is good with people, but man, she couldn't tell you how to properly shut down her computer if her life depended on it!"

When we reinforce stereotypes, all we're doing is reinforcing someone's *inability* to do something. We're telling our technical employees that because they're good with computers, we don't expect them to develop people skills. This seems to be accepted—that IQ and EQ have to be mutually exclusive. If our employees believe leadership thinks they're incapable of learning something new, why should they try?

We *want* our technical staff to develop their people skills so we can all work together more effectively to fight cybercrime. We don't want to accept their skills for what they are—we want them to grow. We expect our sales team to work with technology, so we should expect our technical team to work with people, too.

We spoke about perspective earlier. The argument you may hear from technical staff is, "If I have to learn better people skills, maybe you should learn better technical skills."

This is a valid argument—if you supervise technical staff, just as you expect them to learn some people and business skills, they expect you to learn some technical skills. They don't expect you to be a technical genius, but if you have *some* technical skills, it will go a long way with your technical staff.

Stereotypes are limiting. They also divide us. We need to work *together* to win the war. Reinforcing stereotypes points out our differences and limits our technical employees' individual growth and ability to solve problems together. We need to focus on similarities. A good exercise would be to talk about what happens during a cybersecurity breach with all the staff to see what the real impact may be to everyone in the organization.

PEOPLE SKILLS ARE APPLICABLE EVERYWHERE

Technical people will often tell you (leadership) that it's *your* job to deal with people so they don't have to.

How do you respond to this?

Ask them how many people they deal with on a continual basis. Are they in a relationship? Do they have parents or kids? Are those relationships flourishing? If not, they could benefit from improving their people skills.

People skills are applicable everywhere, not just the workplace. If you can get your technical staff to acknowledge the need for enhanced people skills at home, it might be easier for them to acknowledge those skills are needed at the office, too.

COMPLICATED SOLUTIONS

A lack of acknowledgment bleeds into the way our technical staff solves problems, too. Most of them simply won't acknowledge that their overly complicated solutions are ineffective. This stems from insecurity and fear. The ego takes over and attempts to mask the insecurity and fear. It hides behind the complicated framework.

Many technical employees refuse to acknowledge any solutions or ideas that differ from theirs—remember the CISO who insisted on an overcomplicated and expensive solution versus the simple and much more affordable solution we (Alpine Security) recommended? They refuse to acknowledge simple solutions to complex problems and instead prescribe complicated checklists and convoluted frameworks that only they can understand. If they oversimplify the solution, it will damage their fragile ego. If the solution is simple, they think you won't need their help anymore. Acknowledgment impacts this aspect of cybersecurity, too.

A lack of acknowledgment impacts not only your technical team's ability to do good work and learn new skills, but it also hinders their ability to simplify. They refuse to acknowledge solutions other than their own because complexity is often how they justify their job. Or they don't have the confidence to come up with their own solutions.

If we don't acknowledge our technical teams' accomplishments, how can we expect them to acknowledge anything themselves? How can we expect them to focus on simple solutions when we haven't acknowledged their ability to come up with them?

ENCOURAGE PROFESSIONAL GROWTH

When you think about it, none of us are born experts of anything. We aren't born walking or talking. We have to learn each word and each step. And we need encouragement and acknowledgment along the way. When a baby takes its first steps, everyone in attendance claps. We should treat every new venture the same. We should clap for every major accomplishment.

Acknowledging your technical employees' accomplishments helps you build momentum. (Don't know what to do? Take another look at the 5 Languages of Appreciation.) When you clap for a baby's first step, it tries to take step two. When learning something new, none of us are any different. If your technical staff have already successfully demonstrated they're capable of something tough, it isn't far-fetched to believe they can do it again. That's one of the reasons why David Goggins fills his cookie jar with his accomplishments. He uses it as a reminder that he's capable of anything.

CHEAT SHEET: BUILD RAPPORT

There are a few ways to do this. Here's another:[31]

1. Check your appearance.
2. Remember the basics of good communication.
3. Find common ground.
4. Create shared experiences.
5. Be empathic.
6. Mirror and match mannerisms and speech appropriately.

---

31   "Building Rapport: Establishing Strong Two-Way Connections," MindTools, accessed November 13, 2020, https://www.mindtools.com/pages/article/building-rapport.htm.

When we take the time to acknowledge our technical employees' accomplishments, it's easier to encourage their continued growth, too. You're able to build a positive rapport because they are more likely to like and trust you. You are someone who appreciates them and acknowledges their accomplishments. You aren't just using them like so many other managers have in the past. People like to be around people who make them feel good about themselves.

Many technical employees don't trust corporate leadership, and it causes them to feel disconnected from the organization as a whole. If you take the time to build a rapport, however, they will be more likely to listen to you if you tactfully suggest a change in their behavior.

I want my team to succeed at the highest possible level. For me, success is when I'm no longer needed—when my team can do everything without me and *better* than me. I now like to put myself in situations where I'm the most unintelligent person in the room so I can learn and grow. If you're always the smartest person in the room, you're not going to grow very much, if at all.

Acknowledging the positive things your technical team has done in the past (and continues to do in the present) will open them up to constructive criticism in the future. If you want to get them to improve their people skills tomorrow, you've got to give them a little credit *today*.

TIPS AND TRICKS: HOW TO BUILD RAPPORT QUICKLY

Building rapport with your technical employees isn't easy, but it's *easier* if you acknowledge their accomplishments. (Remember, we aren't trying to build rapport to manipulate people—the intent is to help.)

However, some of us need to build rapport quickly. We don't have time to wait for an accomplishment to acknowledge. We don't have time to wait for another cookie to put inside the jar.

Whenever I train a new group of techs or executives on improving their people skills, I need to build rapport *fast*. I've got to get these people to know, like, and trust me; otherwise, the training will be completely useless. If you're ever in a situation like this, here are a few tactics you can try:

1. **Ask about their hobbies.** Hobbies are one of the many things that make us unique. When you ask someone about their hobby, you learn something about them that others in the group probably don't know. This will help you cultivate trust.
2. **Ask for an interesting fact.** Each and every one of us is interesting. I chose to ride out the first two months of the COVID-19 pandemic in Dublin, Ireland, almost four thousand miles away from home. Knowing that about me creates a connection and instantly builds rapport.
3. **Ask them to name their theme song.** In professional wrestling, boxing, and MMA, each athlete enters the arena to music. This is their theme song. When you ask your technical employees to name theirs, it gives them an opportunity to be creative and form a bond with you.

Building rapport with technical employees isn't easy, but it's a necessary step toward working well together. If you have good rapport with your team, they will be more open to constructive criticism and feedback, and the quality of their work will improve.

BUILD RAPPORT AND TRUST

One of the things I'm relatively obsessed with is marketing, and I think anyone could benefit from Blair Warren's "One-Sentence Persuasion" course. The one sentence is this:

People will do anything for those who encourage their dreams, justify their failures, allay their fears, confirm their suspicions, and help them throw rocks at their enemies.

If you keep this sentence in mind when building rapport with someone, it will help. I'm not suggesting you lie, but if you adhere to the five items in Blair Warren's one sentence as much as you can, your chances of building rapport are better.

Most corporate leaders don't know how to acknowledge the accomplishments of their technical staff. They don't understand the complexities of the industry, so they don't know how to recognize challenges. Without that recognition, their ability to acknowledge good work is severely compromised. This is often because the accomplishments are intangible. Plus, in cybersecurity, many organizations measure success as "we haven't been breached." Success should be based on items that can be measured, not the lack of something happening. It's also worth noting that in cybersecurity we can get 10,000 things right, but the one thing we miss or get wrong, gets noticed. The bad guys, the cybercriminals, have to get only one thing right.

Technical leaders don't know how to acknowledge their technical staff either. They emphasize everything their employees do wrong when they should be focusing on everything they're doing *right*. If you tell a child not to run, they will do just that. Focusing on the negative only breeds more negative behavior. It's a vicious circle.

This impacts the cybersecurity industry because a lack of acknowledgment leaves our technical employees disengaged. We reinforce stereotypes, which forces them to give attention to the wrong things and in turn leads to convoluted solutions only they can understand. It's no wonder we're losing the war.

Like David Goggins's cookie jar tells us, a little bit of acknowledgment goes a long way. Not only will our technical employees' connection to their job, the company, and the cybersecurity industry improve overall, but they will also be more open to feedback. Acknowledgment builds rapport and trust, which are needed if we want to encourage continued growth and change.

We also need to know how to communicate with our technical staff, and our technical staff need to know how to communicate with us. All that and more, coming up next.

EXERCISE: INCREASE ACKNOWLEDGMENT

Acknowledgment and appreciation go hand in hand. Here are two activities you can do with your technical staff to increase their acknowledgment.

Activity 1:
The David Goggins Cookie Jar

We're going to keep this activity short and sweet—we're going to create an acknowledgment cookie jar. David Goggins uses the jar personally (as do I), but I also suggest using it for your technical team.

Overview: Reflecting and annotating the challenges you've already overcome acknowledges what you've already accomplished and gives you something tangible to remind you of what you are capable of.

Objective: To acknowledge what you've already accomplished and build confidence in what you are capable of achieving.

Preparation: Ask your team to think of something they've accomplished in the past week, past month, and past year. Ask them also to think of the biggest accomplishment of their life. This could be the same as one of the first three, but encourage them to come up with something different if possible.*

If your employees struggle with this, they can refer to their employee reviews for help or schedule a time with you to brainstorm.

Materials: Pen, paper, cookie jar.**

***If you don't have a cookie jar (or don't want to be that literal), a container of any kind will do. Just make sure it's big enough for all your "cookies."*

Step 1: During the meeting, ask your team to write down their accomplishments on the scrap pieces of paper. They can add their names or remain anonymous—it's completely up to them.

Step 2: Once they're done writing, explain the purpose of the cookie jar is to acknowledge their accomplishments and see how far they've come as a team.

Step 3: Ask if anyone would like to share their accomplishments. (I recommend starting first to break the ice.) Once everyone who wants to share is finished, ask the group to place their accomplishments in the jar.

Step 4: Display the jar somewhere that's visible to the entire team, and every time someone accomplishes something challenging, acknowledge it by writing it down on a scrap of paper and tossing it into the jar.

Step 5: Whenever anyone on the team is down or feeling discouraged, just refer to the jar to remind them of everything they're capable of based on what they accomplished in the past.

Activity 2:
Open-Ended Questions

The next time you're in a meeting, take a couple of minutes to ask an **open-ended question** of each team member. When you ask an open-ended question, the respondent can't answer with a yes, a no, or a maybe. Open-ended questions require specific answers.

Overview: Open-ended questions give you insight into someone else's perspective, build rapport, and provide insight.

Objective: To build rapport, learn more about a colleague(s) and understand what they appreciate.

Preparation: Think about each member on your team and come up with two open-ended questions you can ask them. (It's best to do this work ahead of time.)

Materials: None.

Step 1: Schedule the meeting.

Step 2: Let your team know the purpose of the meeting.

Step 3: Start asking questions.

What is your favorite movie and what do you like about it?

What is your favorite book and what about it resonates with you?

What do you like most about your role in our organization?

What do you like least about your role in our organization?

How do you define success?

(Remember to avoid asking why questions, as these typically make people defensive.)

In coaching sessions when I ask these types of questions of teams that have worked together for years, I'm always amazed. More often than not, they know nothing of one another's interests because they never built rapport. They never asked each other questions.

Open-ended questions are a fantastic way to learn more about your team, build rapport, and enhance camaraderie.

CHAPTER 6

※ ※ ※

STEP 4: COMMUNICATION

Wise men speak because they have something to say; Fools because they have to say something.

—PLATO

About eight to nine years ago, I was invited to play World of Warcraft, a fantasy-themed computer game, with a bunch of my technical colleagues. I had never played before, but the programmer who invited me insisted I would pick it up quickly. World of Warcraft is a **massively multiplayer online role-playing game (MMORPG)**, and there would be a lot of other people playing who could show me the ropes. So I agreed.

When I started playing with everyone, I quickly realized how advanced they were. I also quickly realized how *well* they were all working together (rather seamlessly, I might add) to solve problems (quests). They were cognizant of their differences, but they also knew that in order to win the game, those differences were necessary. Working together, despite them, was the key to victory. Even though it was "just a game" and the consequences weren't that big of a deal, my technical colleagues had no problem communicating to solve problems.

Witnessing this behavior from my technical peers was eye-opening. Throughout my entire career, I saw technical people struggle to communicate and work with others (nontech and tech) to solve problems. In World of Warcraft, though, they didn't struggle at all. They achieved their objectives with ease. They communicated and worked together effectively, and they enjoyed doing it.

NLP PRESUPPOSITIONS FOR COMMUNICATION

- **Respect for the other person's model of the world.**
- **Resistance is a sign of a lack of rapport.**
  (There are no resistant clients, only inflexible communicators. Effective communicators accept and utilize all communication present to them.)
- **Calibrate on behavior.**
  (The most important information about a person is that person's behavior.)
- **The map is not the territory.**
  (The words we use are NOT the event or the item they represent.)
- **There is ONLY feedback!**
  (There is no failure, only feedback.)
- **The meaning of communication is the response you get.**
- **The law of requisite variety.**
  (The system/person with the most flexibility of behavior will control the system.)

GEEK SPEAK AND ROBOT TALK

There is a communication gap between our technical people and our company leaders, and it's one of the main things responsible for the good guys' current losing streak in the cybersecurity war. There is a communication gap because of **geek speak**, **robot talk**, and **poor listening skills**.

LEETSPEAK

Your technical employees' desire to be part of a "geek subculture" is human nature because significance is often achieved by being something different and unique.

Leetspeak is an internet language that replaces standard letters with numerals and symbols. It was developed in the 1980s—nearly a decade before the introduction of the World Wide Web. After the internet was introduced, hackers used leetspeak to throw search engines off their scent (it worked back then). The hacker language is still used today as a mark of high status and sometimes even by big companies like Google, which many believe is a nod to the underground subculture.[32]

Here is an example of a phrase translated into leetspeak:[33]

hack the planet

h4cK 7h3 Pl4n37

Technical people tend to speak technical jargon so only others in the cybersecurity industry will understand. Sometimes you even have to be in a specific niche of cybersecurity to understand. Penetration testers speak very differently than auditors, as an example. This leads to communication breakdowns and eventually data breaches.

To give you an example, this is a short conversation I had with my CTO the other day:

---

32 "Leetspeak: The History of Hacker Culture's Native Tongue," Alpine Security, accessed November 13, 2020, https://alpinesecurity.com/blog/leetspeak-the-history-of-hacker-culture/.

33 "Me Loved Leetspeak Generator," 1337.me, accessed October 20, 2020, https://1337.me.

"We need to exploit the vulnerability, get a meterpreter shell, then run Mimikatz."

"Do we need to kill AV before priv esc?"

This is "robot talk" or "geek speak," and it's completely unintelligible to everyone (outside of the industry) who hears it. A nurse friend of mine used to hear me talk on the phone a lot to my team. She said she couldn't understand anything I said and referred to it as "robot talk." It's as if an entire subculture has formed—technical people want to engage in geek speak so others *won't* understand them. The robot talk is on purpose.

This primarily goes back to technical people's insecurities and fears. If others understand what they're talking about, their convoluted—and potentially ineffective—solutions will be exposed. Technical people resist changing their communication patterns because they're afraid everyone will discover their superspecial language isn't actually all that special after all.

And it really isn't. I'm not trying to downplay the amount of work it takes to achieve success in this industry or the intellect it takes to comprehend cybersecurity concepts and theories, but the use of the obscure naming conventions and geek speak are often unnecessary. Cybersecurity is no longer a subculture. It's actually quite mainstream, as it affects most businesses and we hear about it on the news daily.

There is *always* a way to simplify language in order to communicate more effectively, but most technical people don't take the initiative to make those changes. If business leaders don't understand them, they don't care. They think everyone should be able to understand cybersecurity; if they can't, they must not be that smart or they "just don't get it."

And if technical people don't value your intellectual level, they're going to be even *less* likely to alter their communication (and word choice) so that you understand. It's a perpetual problem.

FOUR PAGES OF ACRONYMS

One of the foundational cybersecurity certifications is CompTIA Security+. This certification is difficult and becoming even more so as CompTIA attempts to make the exam more "simulation-based" in order to eliminate the paper tigers.

The high-level objectives for the Security+ exam cover quite a few areas of cybersecurity:

- Threats, Attacks, and Vulnerabilities
- Architecture and Design
- Implementation
- Operations and Incident Response
- Governance, Risk, and Compliance

That list of objectives is simple enough. What isn't is the list of acronyms test takers are required to know in order to take the exam. As an example, this is what's included on the first page:

Security+ (SY0-601) Acronym List

The following is a list of acronyms that appear on the CompTIA Security+ exam.
Candidates are encouraged to review the complete list and attain a working knowledge
of all listed acronyms as part of a comprehensive exam preparation program.

ACRONYM	DEFINITION
3DES	Triple Digital Encryption Algorithm
AAA	Authentication, Authorization, and Accounting
ABAC	Attribute-based Access Control
ACL	Access Control List
AD	Active Directory
AES	Advanced Encryption Standard
AES256	Advanced Encryption Standards 256bit
AH	Authentication Header
AI	Artificial Intelligence
AIS	Automated Indicator Sharing
ALE	Annualized Loss Expectancy
AP	Access Point
API	Application Programming Interface
APT	Advanced Persistent Threat
ARO	Annualized Rate of Occurrence
ARP	Address Resolution Protocol
ASLR	Address Space Layout Randomization
ASP	Active Server Pages
ATT&CK	Adversarial Tactics, Techniques, and Common Knowledge
AUP	Acceptable Use Policy
AV	Antivirus
BASH	Bourne Again Shell
BCP	Business Continuity Planning
BGP	Border Gateway Protocol

BIA	Business Impact Analysis
BIOS	Basic Input/Output System
BPA	Business Partnership Agreement
BPDU	Bridge Protocol Data Unit
BSSID	Basic Service Set Identifier
BYOD	Bring Your Own Device
CA	Certificate Authority
CAC	Common Access Card
CAPTCHA	Completely Automated Public Turing Test to Tell Computers and Humans Apart
CAR	Corrective Action Report
CASB	Cloud Access Security Broker
CBC	Cipher Block Chaining
CBT	Computer-based Training
CCMP	Counter-Mode/CBC-MAC Protocol
CCTV	Closed-Circuit Television
CERT	Computer Emergency Response Team
CFB	Cipher Feedback
CHAP	Challenge-Handshake Authentication Protocol
CIO	Chief Information Officer
CIRT	Computer Incident Response Team
CIS	Center for Internet Security
CMS	Content Management System
CN	Common Name
COOP	Continuity of Operations Planning
COPE	Corporate-owned Personally Enabled
CP	Contingency Planning
CRC	Cyclic Redundancy Check

Security+ (SY0-601) Acronym List

CRL	Certificate Revocation List
CSA	Cloud Security Alliance
CSIRT	Computer Security Incident Response Team
CSO	Chief Security Officer
CSP	Cloud Service Provider
CSR	Certificate Signing Request
CSRF	Cross-Site Request Forgery
CSU	Channel Service Unit
CTM	Counter-Mode
CTO	Chief Technology Officer
CVE	Common Vulnerabilities and Exposures
CVSS	Common Vulnerability Scoring System
CYOD	Choose Your Own Device
DAC	Discretionary Access Control
DBA	Database Administrator
DDoS	Distributed Denial-of-Service
DEP	Data Execution Prevention

Cybersecurity certifications require you to memorize long lists of acronyms.

No wonder we have robot talk and geek speak—we teach people to use these acronyms and then test them on how well they know them.

POOR LISTENING SKILLS

I talked about this at the very beginning of the book, but it's worth mentioning again. Communication isn't only about the words we use; it's about our tone of voice and body language, too. To remind you:

MEHRABIAN'S 7-38-55 THEORY OF COMMUNICATIONS

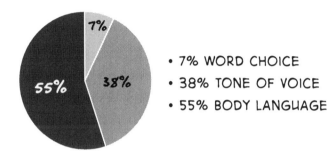

- 7% WORD CHOICE
- 38% TONE OF VOICE
- 55% BODY LANGUAGE

Communication is mostly about our body language and tone of voice. It has very little to do with the words we use.[34]

Effective, productive communication is also about how well we listen. In today's digital age, many of us are poor listeners. We aren't present in the moment when someone is speaking to us—we're thinking about something else. Either that or we're on our phones or tablets. And we're all culprits of this. It isn't just the technical folk.

People also tend to listen for agreement (or ammunition, as a friend of mine says) rather than insight (we've talked about this before, too). They look for a place to insert themselves into the conversation rather than work to understand where the other person is coming from. They simply wait to interject.

---

34   Nagesh Belludi, "Albert Mehrabian's 7-38-55 Rule of Personal Communication," Right Attitudes, October 4, 2008, https://www.rightattitudes. com/2008/10/04/7-38-55-rule-personal-communication/.

This impacts our relationships, our companies, and the industry as a whole because when we don't actively listen, we can't fully understand the problem. If we're only listening for agreement, we're missing opportunities for insight. Our clients need us to help them, not agree (or disagree, unless it's helpful) with them. When we don't listen, we can't understand the problem and thus, can't offer relevant, impactful solutions. Try to recall the last time you spoke with a salesperson and they did all the talking without listening to what you needed.

THE IMPACT ON CYBERSECURITY

When there is a communication gap between technical employees and company leadership, the proper decisions aren't made. This is how a lack of effective communication impacts the cybersecurity industry.

If technical people refuse to alter their language to effectively communicate with company management, how can they expect leadership to understand their problems and provide well-thought-out solutions or a budget, which is often the complaint? I have seen this play out time and time again in cybersecurity, especially with some of the highest-ranking technical leaders. I once witnessed a CISO give a presentation to a board of directors, but the presentation was so technical that no one on the board understood what he was talking about. When I asked him about it, he said, "They just didn't get it." However, the point of these meetings and presentations *is* for them to "get it." Otherwise, it's just a waste of everyone's time.

Cybersecurity should be explained in terms of risk to the business, not in technical jargon.

We, as leaders, want to understand the information our technical team is presenting. We want to make informed decisions to best protect our data, and we can only do that if we understand the language used to describe what's technically occurring.

Because most company leaders don't understand geek speak, though, the expectation isn't on them to alter their communication style—the expectation is on the technical side. Technical employees must be able to alter *their* communication to talk to corporate leadership. It simply cannot be the other way around.

Technical leaders and employees can't expect a company executive to understand what "we have 100s of servers vulnerable to EternalBlue" means. They didn't get certified or earn a degree in cybersecurity. They don't have experience in the field; their technical team members do. That's why company leadership relies on them to secure their data—management is well aware of the fact they don't have the technical chops to do it themselves. It's the responsibility of the technical community to improve their communication with nontechnical people, not the other way around. The effect of EternalBlue, for instance, should be explained in terms or real risk to the business, steps that can be taken to mitigate the risk, and the resources required to take those steps.

This is really no different than when you visit a doctor. When you see a doctor, they explain things to you in a manner you understand. Well, the best doctors do this.

THE DIFFERENCE BETWEEN LEFT- AND RIGHT-BRAINED PEOPLE

Your technical employees often don't want to alter their communication style to be more effective because it's challenging in a nontangible manner. It's much harder than learning a new programming language (for instance) because the latter is a finite activity. There is a definitive beginning, middle, and end.

Programming languages are also black and white. There are clear, delineated steps that tell the student exactly what to do and how to move through the process. Formulaic processes like this appeal to left-brained people, like your technical team. They are logical and very good at repeating a set order of tasks, but they usually aren't very adaptable, especially when it comes to solutions that are not "if-then-else." An if-then-else solution is black and white—if this happens, do that; otherwise (else), do this. People don't work this way and there are too many unknown variables, such as the context or the person. If "this" happens with one person, you may do "X." If the same thing happens with another person, you may need to do "Y." Knowing when to apply X or Y is the challenge.

Communication is ever changing because each of us is different. Being a successful communicator requires flexibility. You have to be able to adapt to new people and new situations and do it quickly. Creative, right-brained types seem to have no problem with this, but technical people do because they typically have a harder time adapting.

Let me give you an example. If you were to dig a ditch, you would use one tool—a shovel—because that's all you need to dig a ditch. It's a very straightforward task. Planting a garden, however, is much more complicated. You need a hoe, a rake, and maybe pruning shears. You also probably need a watering can. There are many more tools to manage when planting a garden, and for technical people, managing that many may be overwhelming. They don't know how to easily switch between tools and tasks to accomplish the objective, so it wouldn't be easy for them to plant a garden. They would often rather dig a ditch. The variables are less for the ditch and the measurements for success have more clarity.

BEHAVIORAL FLEXIBILITY

The idea of **behavioral flexibility** is big in NLP. In order to get a desired result, we have to alter our behavior to match the situation.

The same goes for communication. I don't talk to a five-year-old the same way I talk to a fifty-year-old, and I don't talk to the technical team the same way I talk to the sales team.

SHARED LANGUAGES LEAD TO SUCCESS

We've seen two examples that illustrate the importance of speaking a common language. Remember when I explained my company's financials to Karen using the language she speaks, she understood the situation and wanted to be part of the solution. Likewise, when the board didn't understand the CISO's message, he left the meeting frustrated—and we can imagine the board felt frustrated and confused, too. Executives, technical leaders, and the technical staff—not to mention the cybersecurity industry as a whole—share the common goal of wanting to solve problems and protect data from the bad guys, but if we don't communicate effectively and we don't understand the business risk, we struggle to provide the technical team with the resources they need to do their job well.

Poor communication can also lead to big problems such as medical device hacking or data breaches. Breakdowns, simply because technical people refuse to communicate in a way that nontechnical people can understand, can be devastating to a company. Errors like these can lead to lawsuits, a damaged reputation, and financial ruin. Use of a shared language as well as active listening leads to more effective communication, which enables corporate leaders *and* technical employees to succeed.

SENSORY DATA

In NLP, effective communication is measured by the result you get from the other person. If they understand you and are moved to action, your communication was effective. If it leads to an argument, it was *in*effective.

Many people don't look at communication this way. They don't see it as something that generates "results," but it does. Communication drives action.

It's easiest to see this play out with the words. What we hear on the radio, see on the television, or read on the internet has the power to influence us to take action or live in fear. It could be an ad, a newscast, or an article. Words have the power to communicate a call to action rather easily.

However, communication isn't just the words we see and hear. According to NLP, there are five ways to receive sensory data:

1. Visual (what we see)
2. Kinesthetic (what we feel)
3. Auditory (what we hear)
4. Olfactory (what we smell)
5. Gustatory (what we taste)

Language and communication is the processing of sensory data. At any given moment, we receive over a million bits of info per second. However, our brains can process only about 150 bits per second, meaning our brains are constantly deleting, distorting, and generalizing data received. Of course there is great variability in what these numbers actually are, but the reality is, there is much more sensory data hitting us than we can process, so our coping mechanisms is to delete, distort, or generalize (DDG).

We each have our own DDG filter, meaning we all process information differently. So why do we expect everyone to experience the world the way we do?

NLP COMMUNICATION MODEL

INTERNAL REPRESENTATION

FILTERS
VALUES
BELIEFS
META PROGRAMS
DECISIONS
MEMORIES

STATE

PHYSIOLOGY

NLP META MODEL
DELETE
DISTORT
GENERALIZE

← OVER 1 Mʙᴘꜱ (MEGABIT PER SECOND)
EXTERNAL EVENT
(NLP REP. SYSTEM)
← VISUAL
← AUDITORY
← KINESTHETIC
← OLFACTORY
← GUSTATORY

OUTPUT
OUR BEHAVIOR

We cannot process all the data we receive, so we delete, distort, and generalize as well as apply additional filters. This is why two people can witness the same event, yet recall and react completely differently.

Some of the more traumatic of this filtered sense data turns into the programs we've been talking about throughout the book, and certain sensory data triggers (starts) these programs. Typically, these types of programs are imprinted on us before age seven and play out our entire lives.

Doug, for example, was picked on by his older brothers when he was a kid. They beat him up and called him stupid. Because of it, he *still* strives to be the smartest person in the room—and he's in his fifties. He wants to call other people "stupid" because that's how he was treated as a child. Whenever he feels dumb, this program is triggered, and he spends the rest of the day trying to find a way to call the other person (the one who made him feel dumb) stupid.

Does this sound like an effective method of communication? No, it sounds like being a bully—and nobody likes a bully, let alone wants to work with one. Bullies were typically bullied. Bullying is quite rampant in technical fields, especially cybersecurity. A friend and colleague of mine, Marilise de Villiers, an executive in cybersecurity, wrote the book *ROAR! How to Tame the Bully Inside and Out* about this concept.

ALTER YOUR COMMUNICATION

To achieve results, technical people must alter their communication with corporate leadership. They can do this by simplifying their language (there is always a way), recognizing the leadership team's learning style, and building rapport.

NLP can help with all of that. It's already helped with awareness (territory maps) and mindset (cause vs. effect), and it can help with communication, too.

Specifically, NLP suggests specific word choices can point to an individual's **learning style**. People tend to be kinesthetic, auditory, or visual learners. Framing communication around the listener's learning style makes it easier for them to understand and then take action.

For instance, if someone you know uses phrases like "I feel you" or "I got a grip on that," they are probably a kinesthetic learner. Someone who says "I hear you" is probably an auditory learner, whereas someone who says "I see that" probably learns visually.

Understanding how someone best absorbs new information (i.e., their learning style) makes it easier to communicate with them.

NLP offers terrific tactics for building rapport. One is called **matching** and the other, **mirroring**.

When you match, you copy the other person's words and/or gestures. If they put their left hand on their hip, put your left hand on your hip, too. If they use a specific word, you use it, too. (Not right away, though. You don't want to make it too obvious. Wait a little bit first.)

Mirroring is when you alter the gestures and/or words slightly. If they put their left hand on their hip, put your *right* hand on your hip. Do (or say) something similar.

Many studies show that people feel more comfortable around people who use similar gestures and/or vocabulary, which makes it easier to build rapport. After I learned this technique, I tried it with complete strangers, and it was much easier to talk to them. Matching and mirroring are excellent techniques for building rapport.

TIPS AND TRICKS: REFRAME THE OBJECTIVE

When I was in Italy a few years ago, I witnessed an American (who didn't speak any Italian) try to order ice cream from an Italian who didn't speak a lot of English. The American repeated his order over and over again, getting louder each time it was evident the Italian couldn't understand him. He didn't try to place his order differently or even bother to look up the words in Italian—he raised his voice instead.

A measure of effective communication is its result. If you communicate effectively, the listener will understand and, if necessary, take action.

Most technical employees don't know how to or don't want to learn how to communicate effectively, and the cybersecurity industry suffers. Poor communication impacts their ability to work together to solve problems. Data breaches and medical device hacks are a result of poor communication.

Deep down, these people know they need to improve their communication, but they're afraid. They're afraid they'll be exposed for their lack of knowledge. If they aren't afraid, they aren't willing to put in the work. It's hard to change communication patterns. It's possible but takes focus and commitment. A lot of commitment...Just today, I found myself running an old routine—one of those neural pathways I thought I'd removed. Even though I knew the program was running, I was having trouble stopping it. I had to take a deep breath, zoom out, and disassociate myself from the situation. This allowed me to gain perspective, think about what really mattered, and hit a CTRL-C on the program to kill it. This is not an easy thing to do.

There are a couple of additional tips I can give you to help strengthen your technical team's communication skills.

1. **Revisit awareness.** Good communication means good listening skills and understanding the other person's point of view. This all starts with awareness. If your technical people are aware, they need to put themselves in the other person's shoes. Encourage your technical staff to raise awareness to improve their communication skills.
2. **Reframe the objective.** Here's something else you can try. We talked about this throughout the chapter, but most people don't realize that communication is actually results driven. We can easily measure its effectiveness by how the person we're communicating

with responds. For some of your technical staff, when you reframe the objective like this, the importance of communication becomes apparent.

SIMPLIFY THE MESSAGE

In World of Warcraft, the need for communication is inherent—it just "clicks." The players all know they need to work together in order to win and that diversity is the key.

Those communication skills don't seem to transfer over to the real world, however, and the cybersecurity industry suffers for it. Miscommunication leads to data breaches and ineffective cybersecurity controls—it's one of the main reasons why we're losing the war.

There is *always* a way to communicate and work together because there's *always* a way to simplify the message so it's easier for others to understand. In this case, it means changing the vernacular and refraining from geek speak and robot talk when communicating with executives. It also means listening for insight, rather than agreement, and building rapport.

Once you've got communication down, it's time to move on to the next step in the methodology, monotasking. I'll tell you what that has to do with winning the cybersecurity war next.

EXERCISE: ENHANCE COMMUNICATION

To win the cybersecurity war (and our own internal war), effective communication is key. Here are two activities to help you and your technical staff enhance communication.

Activity 1:
Eye Patterns

There is another cool communication hack in NLP and it has to do with eye patterns. Maybe you've heard of this, but you can tell whether or not someone is lying by the direction of their eyes. If you ask them a question and they look left, they are recalling information that's real and accurate. They're telling you the truth. If they look to the right, they are creating information and are therefore lying.

The eyes are the closest organ to the brain, and they actually "look" toward where they're trying to access information. If they look to the left, they are looking at the left and logical side of the brain, the side of the brain that recalls memory. If they look to the right, they are looking at the creative, storytelling side of the brain.

Overview: Eye patterns can provide insight into how someone processes information—are they visual, auditory, or kinesthetic? Eye patterns can also give you insight into whether someone is remembering or creating.

Objective: To understand how to read people better when communicating with them, and to understand how people process information and if they are creating or remembering what they are telling you.

Preparation: Make copies of the diagram on the following page to distribute to your team *at the end of the activity*. (For a digital copy, visit www.christianespinosa.com/spitr/resources.)

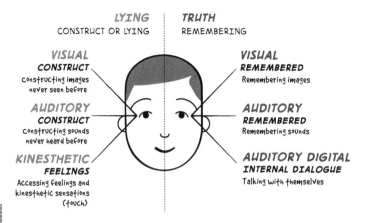

LYING | TRUTH
CONSTRUCT OR LYING | REMEMBERING

VISUAL
CONSTRUCT
Constructing images
never seen before

VISUAL
REMEMBERED
Remembering images

AUDITORY
CONSTRUCT
Constructing sounds
never heard before

AUDITORY
REMEMBERED
Remembering sounds

KINESTHETIC
FEELINGS
Accessing feelings and
kinesthetic sensations
(touch)

AUDITORY DIGITAL
INTERNAL DIALOGUE
Talking with themselves

If someone looks left, they are remembering. I always remember if I am looking at someone and they look right (from my perspective), they are remembering, telling the truth.[35]

Materials: Pen and paper, diagram copies.

Step 1: Ask your technical employees to partner up.

Step 2: Ask them each to write down three short stories—two made-up/constructed and one truthful/remembered.

Step 3: Ask partner 1 to tell partner 2, from memory, their three short stories in any order. Tell them not to reveal which are constructed and which is remembered.

Step 4: Ask partner 2 to watch the eye direction of partner 1 when they say their statements. Ask partner 2 to write down the eye direction for each statement.

Step 5: Ask the partners to switch places. Then repeat the process.

35 Janey Davies, "Eye Movements When Lying: Reality of Myth?" Learning Mind, February 19, 2018, https://www.learning-mind.com/eye-movements-when-lying/.

Step 6: When both partners have said each of their three statements, tell them that a look to the left means it was remembered, and a look to the right means it was constructed. Ask each partner to reveal whether their statements were remembered or constructed, and see how well the eye patterns match up.

This is a fun little tip anyone can use to improve their communication skills.

Activity 2:
Matching and Mirroring

People feel more comfortable around others who use similar gestures and/or vocabulary, making matching and mirroring excellent techniques for building rapport. Matching means doing something similar but slightly different (I sit with my right leg over my left leg; you sit with your right foot over your left foot). Mirroring means doing the same thing—a "mirror image" (I sit with my right leg over my left leg; you sit with your right leg over your left leg). Next time you meet a new client or a new person for coffee, try matching and mirroring them some to see how it affects rapport. You can even try this on a sales call (or on company meetings) over Zoom.

Overview: Building rapport is easier when you and the person you're building rapport with are similar. People generally like people who are like them, which makes communication easier and more effective.

Objective: To quickly build rapport with someone in order to improve communication.

Preparation: No prep is needed for this activity.

Materials: Pen and paper.

Step 1: Schedule a call with a new client.

Step 2: Choose either matching or mirroring.

If you chose **matching**...

Step 3: During the meeting, jot down words or phrases the new client uses.

Step 4: Incorporate those words and phrases into your contribution to the conversation. For example, if the client uses the word *execute* when describing the problem they need help solving, use *execute* to describe the solution.

If you chose **mirroring**...

Step 3: During the meeting, pay attention to your client's gestures and mannerisms. Do they talk with their hands? Or are they still and motionless but give an occasional head nod?

Step 4: Whatever the gestures are, mirror them. If your client talks with their hands, talk with *your* hands. If all they do is head nod, that's all you should do, too.

Matching and mirroring is a fun and easy way to build rapport with people you don't know very well. I recommend trying this one in your personal life, too!

CHAPTER 7

▓ ▓ ▓

STEP 5: MONOTASKING

Multitasking is the opportunity to screw up more than one thing at a time.

—UNKNOWN

In 2016, my work life was imbalanced. I was a new business owner (and a new CEO), and my time was hijacked all day, every day. My phone rang off the hook, emails popped up constantly, and there was always a small fire to put out at the office.

I wanted to grow my business, but I was a slave to everyone else's time. I couldn't focus on any of my own initiatives because I was too busy helping everyone else. It impacted my mental presence in meetings, affected the quality of my work, and added stress to my life. I was like Popeye in need of that miraculous can of spinach, but I needed to strengthen my time management skills...and I needed to do it miraculously fast.

I read *Living with a SEAL: 31 Days Training with the Toughest Man on the Planet* by Jesse Itzler. The SEAL in the book is actually David Goggins, whom I previously mentioned. I then read *Living with the Monks: What Turning Off My Phone Taught*

Me about Happiness, Gratitude, and Focus by Jesse Itzler. It's a story about Itzler's time living in the New Skete Monastery in Cambridge, New York.[36] I wasn't sure how a story about monks could help me with time management, but something shifted after I read (well, I listened to it on audible.com) *Living with the Monks*. I think I had heard of monotasking before, but something about the way Itzler described it provided more clarity.

There was one passage in particular that stuck out. It was a story about Itzler's first assignment training a New Skete Monastery German shepherd named Rainbow. New Skete Monastery is known for their German shepherds, and their dogs are known to be some of the best trained German shepherds in the world.

When Itzler was asked to help train Rainbow, he accepted, but when he showed up to help, he was surprised to find out the monk didn't want his help teaching Rainbow any new tricks (that's the idea Itzler had in his head). Instead, he wanted Itzler to try and *distract* the dog.

So Itzler tried everything he could think of to distract Rainbow. He yelled and screamed and made fart sounds. He ran this way and that...But no matter what he did, *nothing* worked. Itzler couldn't do anything to distract Rainbow. The dog was like a Buckingham Palace guard on duty—it didn't move a muscle.

NLP PRESUPPOSITIONS FOR MONOTASKING

- **People are not their behaviors.**
  (Accept the person; change the behavior.)
- **You are in charge of your mind and therefore your results.**

---

36   New Skete Monasteries (website), accessed November 13, 2020, https://newskete.org/.

(I am also in charge of my mind and therefore my results.)
- **People have all the resources they need to succeed and to achieve their desired outcomes.**
(There are no unresourceful people, only unresourceful states.)

A SLAVE TO EVERYONE ELSE'S TIME

How many of us are like Rainbow? How many of us have laser focus and are impervious to distractions? How many of us are intentional with our time and prefer productivity over busyness. Don't confuse motion with progress, as they say.

Back in 2016, I would have answered "not me" to each of those questions. At the time, I was brainwashed to believe multitasking was the way to go, so I was a slave to my email, my phone, and my text messages. I was a slave to everyone else's time. This worked for a while—I was able to brute force my way through the day. Brute force is not a sustainable strategy, though, especially if you want to grow.

When we multitask, we put everyone else's needs first. We've been trained to answer texts, emails, and instant messages, well, *instantly*, and we've been brainwashed into thinking we're getting more done this way when exactly the opposite is true. If you have to stop a mindful task to answer an email or a phone call, you have to switch from one subject to another. You have to reset your brain and pick up where you left off, causing you to lose time. This is called **context switching** and it is inefficient.

Concentrated effort is more effective than bouncing back and forth between tasks. When the entire day is spent multitasking, only small tasks get done. For big project work or creative work, you need to find time to focus, without distractions, for at least an hour at a time. You need to channel your inner New Skete Monastery German shepherd Rainbow, and do the opposite of multitasking. You need to focus on one thing at a time and **monotask**.

HUMANS WEREN'T BORN TO MULTITASK

Humans weren't born to multitask. When you think about it, the brain isn't capable of processing more than one emotion at a time. If you think about something that makes you angry, you're going to feel angry. If you think of something that makes you happy, you're going to be happy. You might be able to switch back and forth between the two emotions quickly, but you aren't *processing* them at the same time. You're processing one emotion (anger), then the other (happiness).

Our brains are predisposed to process one thing at a time. When we multitask, we context switch and greatly lose productivity during these context switches.

THE IMPACT ON CYBERSECURITY

The cybersecurity industry is littered with people trying to multitask. If you're not sure what I'm talking about, just look for the person hiding behind an array of monitors. I can almost guarantee that person is technical and loves to multitask.

Doug had six monitors at his desk. They were each on a different monitor arm and created a visual barrier between him and the guy he shared a workspace with. (How can you be the smartest person in the room without the most monitors in the room?)

There was always something running on each monitor to justify its need. On one monitor, he had email and on another, his instant message apps. He had one with a web browser and another with utilities, like a calculator and a metric conversion tool. He also used one for programming.

I walked by his desk one day and asked about that last one, the sixth monitor.

"That one is measuring my CPU usage."

"Why are you monitoring that?" I asked.

"Because if malware is launched, I'll know immediately," he said.

He had his finger on the pulse of just about everything (at least he thought he did), but his ability to focus and get things done suffered.

Multitasking plagues the cybersecurity industry and society in general, and no one can get anything done. No one is present anymore. Context switching is sucking up too much time and preventing us from focusing on anything, which is a big problem. We believe we're focusing on everything, but in reality, we focus on nothing. Multitasking is bad for the industry because it causes anxiety in technical employees and negatively impacts their presence and adversely affects their work quality.

ANXIETY

Multitasking causes anxiety because you're always on the edge, as if you're going to miss something. If the phone rings, you've got to answer it. If an email comes in, you've got to read it and respond. You treat each instance like you would an emergency.

How many *real* emergencies do you have each day? For that matter, how many do you have each *year*? For most of us, it's only a few, but everyone acts as if each incoming request is an emergency, and *that* gives us anxiety.

Anxiety prevents us from doing our best work because we're preoccupied with whatever stresses us. When we are in a primal state instead of a powerful one, it's difficult to make good decisions or solve problems. How can we give it our all if we're always waiting to answer the phone or respond to an email?

In cybersecurity, this is especially problematic because the industry is stressful enough as it is. When you're responsible for protecting personal consumer data or a lifesaving medical device, you don't need the extra stress and anxiety of being a slave to your devices, apps, and media. If anything, you need exactly the opposite.

SOME PEOPLE PANIC WHEN THE PHONE RINGS

A few years ago, I was in line waiting to check into a hotel. There were a few people ahead of me, but the line was at a standstill because the front desk clerk kept answering the phone.

After a while of this, I decided to call the hotel myself. When she answered, I told her I was waiting in line (she looked up and I gave her a little wave) and should have priority over people who call in.

She told me it was company policy to answer the phone after three rings, which made zero sense to me. I could tell answering the phone with people in line was stressing her out, so I didn't press it and instead thanked her and hung up.

LACK OF PRESENCE

The inability to "give it our all" ties into a lack of presence. When we multitask, we aren't really present because we're preoccupied—emphasis on *pre*. We're thinking about the request that could be coming from our phone or inbox at any minute. We're thinking about the million other things we have to do because that's how our brains work. We're multitaskers, right? We do a million things at the same time, so it makes sense that we're thinking about a million different things, too.

If we're thinking about a million different things, we can't be present. We can't give whatever it is we're doing (or whomever we're talking to) our full attention. The brain can process only one thing at a time, remember, so it's literally impossible.

Like lack of awareness and poor communication, multitasking impacts the cybersecurity industry. When an individual isn't present, they can't listen, so it's impractical to think they will be able to work together with others to solve problems. They are too busy thinking about all the things to do instead of working on the one thing that matters most. A lack of presence is yet another reason why cybercriminals are winning.

Photographer Eric Pickersgill did an excellent job capturing this idea on film. In his photography series "Removed," he highlights the impact technology has had on the human connection by removing devices from pictures of everyday life—he photoshops the devices out of the images.[37]

In the photographs, the people are right next to each other but

---

37   "Removed" [photography series], Eric Pickersgill Studio, accessed November 13, 2020, https://www.ericpickersgill.com/removed.

aren't looking at or interacting with each other at all. They are completely consumed by their devices.

And what's even worse, no one looks happy in these images. They look disconnected and *sad*. Everyone thinks multitasking is a great thing, but I think it's like this photography exhibit— sad and disconnected. Remember earlier we spoke about how feeling disconnected leads to depression and addiction.

LACK OF QUALITY

Cybercriminals are also winning because multitasking deteriorates quality. If you're working on an email, for example, but then answer the phone when it rings (and then chat with a coworker who stops by), chances are, you're going to make a mistake in the email. When you multitask, your brain naturally combines information but without you being aware of it. If you're trying to send an email but get distracted by other things, you may send the email to the wrong person or forget to enable a firewall rule.

With the amount of sensitive information cybersecurity experts work with every day, it's clear why multitasking and the inherent, inevitable mistakes that happen are a problem. If you send something sensitive to the wrong recipient, you could cause a major security breach, and well, I don't need to tell you what happens next.

Here's another example for you. Let's say your technical employee is responsible for blocking all system ports (openings). If they multitask, they may make a mistake and leave all the ports open instead of blocked and then forget to go back and fix their mistake. Unfortunately, I've seen both scenarios play out dozens of times, and each time it was because of multitasking.

WHAT IS MONOTASKING?

When our technical employees multitask, they try to complete all one hundred checklist items at the same time. Is it better to have one hundred items at 5 percent completion or one item at 100 percent completion? Most technical teams opt for the 5-percent-completion scenario, and this is why we're getting killed in the cyberwar. We need to give attention to what's most critical and work on that to completion first. We need to look at risk and prioritize accordingly.

At the beginning of this chapter, I told you that my work life was imbalanced. I was a slave to everyone else's time (and never focused on my own initiatives) because I was a grade-A multitasker. I was trying to do everything at the same time, and it was killing me. Not only that, I wasn't getting anything substantial done.

That changed after I read *Living with Monks*. I saw the value (the necessity, really) of focusing on one task at a time—I saw the value of monotasking.

Monotasking isn't defined in the *Merriam-Webster* dictionary—yet. It *is* defined in the *Urban Dictionary*, though, and looks like this:

Monotasking: The performance by an individual of one task, and only one task, at a point in time. Monotasking can be more productive than multitasking because it allows an individual to put all their attention and focus on the task at hand. This allows fewer mistakes than would be made if the individual were multitasking.[38]

To be clear, monotasking doesn't mean focusing on one task

---

38 Urban Dictionary, s.v. "Monotasking," accessed June 1, 2020, https://www.urbandictionary.com/define.php?term=monotasking.

or project for eighty hours straight; it means focusing on only one task or project for at least an hour. It means distraction-free focus. You can still work on multiple projects if you monotask; you just focus on one at a time.

When I was first introduced to monotasking, I wasn't so sure. It went against everything I had been corporately groomed to believe was important. For the sake of my business, I had to try something different. The brute-force tactic was no longer working. I needed to be more productive and more efficient, so I started to focus on monotasking. It took me a long time to unlearn all my multitasking bad habits (it was a tough challenge), but it has been worth it.

We are *all* conditioned to believe we have to respond to email and text messages instantly. When the phone rings, most of us stop everything we're doing to answer it. Multitasking has proven detrimental to the success of the cybersecurity industry overall, so it's time to try something new. It's time to try monotasking.

TIPS AND TRICKS: DEVICE-FREE MEETINGS

If you don't know how to get started monotasking, here are some tips. I find it's easiest to start with behavioral expectations for internal and external meetings. As a company leader, this is something you can easily request and reinforce. People should be present and focused in meetings—they shouldn't be on their phones or computers; they should be listening and participating. If they aren't, there's no point to meeting.

At my company, phones aren't allowed in meetings, and if I can tell someone isn't being present, I'll call them out. I'm a believer that people get in life what they tolerate. People are expected to be present. Meetings are for information sharing and brainstorming. I need my team present; I don't need them thinking about the million things they have to do.

I also realize a meeting infers a dialogue, not a monologue. If what needs to be stated is a one-way feed, a monologue, you are better off sending an email, Slack message, or recording a video and sharing the link. It's a waste of time to have a meeting that isn't a dialogue.

It's a little trickier in a post-pandemic workplace where a lot of employees work from home and telecommute to their meetings, but here's a little tip. I had my team on Zoom to go over some numbers and I could tell one of my employees wasn't present. He wasn't moving his eyes, but his computer screen was being reflected in the lenses of his glasses, and I could see him toggling from window to window. His computer's camera was picking up everything on his eyeglass lenses. He thought he was sly, but he was obviously multitasking. Multitasking is a thing of the past, and I've moved on and expect others to move on as well.

BLOCK TIME

My favorite way to monotask is to use a tactic called **block time.** Instead of checking my email every five minutes and answering every phone call, I set aside specific time for these tasks. I also set aside specific time for my project work, which is key. This is how I'm able to work on and complete big projects.

You should schedule block time into your calendar, just like meetings with staff, prospects, and clients. Otherwise, you'll never get to it. It should actually look like a block of time on your calendar.

Completing big project work takes careful planning. When you set your goals for the year, you then have to determine what you need to do to reach them. I prefer to go backward.

To reach your goals for the year, you have to figure out what you need to accomplish each quarter. From there, you need to establish what needs to happen each month, each week, and each day. Once you do, you will know approximately how many hours per day you need to dedicate to the project in order to complete it by the end of the year. Another great reason to do this reverse planning is to determine if your timeline is realistic. Let's say you have a project that you break out all the tasks on and think it will take 600 hours to complete. This doesn't seem like much—600 hours. If you have 8 hours to dedicate to the project per week, that's 75 weeks—nearly 1.5 years. So if you want to complete the project quicker, you need to block out more time per week or find a way to delegate chunks of it. I used to think I could accomplish way more than I thought I could until I started estimating projects, working backward, and seeing realistically how many hours per week I could dedicate to them.

I was able to write this book using this process. I set aside a certain number of hours each week in order to get it done. If I had let any of these blocked time slots slip, it would have taken me longer to get it published. If I had let too many of the time slots slip, I may not have finished the book at all. If you let your block time slots slip, your big project work simply won't get done.

Most technical people are so busy multitasking that they forget to set aside time each day to work on their big projects, the projects that move the needle for them or their organization. Either that or they push their project work to the back burner to put out fires, or work on small, inconsequential tasks, which is even worse. They don't schedule block time to get their project work done, so they get overrun by other people's demands. There will always be fires to put out, but if the same fire keeps flaring back up, this means you haven't found the source, which is typically a lack of process, inadequate training, or the wrong resource.

And this happens to all of us. We wake up and check our email and text messages—all before we think about our day. Then, before we know it, the day is over and we feel like we didn't get anything done because we didn't. Nothing big anyway. Being busy doesn't mean you're being productive.

Every day (well, most days—I'm not perfect), I wake up and set my agenda. I take into consideration my goals and big project work and create block time slots throughout my day. I have only one rule: the blocks need to be at least 45 minutes in length. You should plan 5 to 10 minutes between your blocks. These 5 to 10 minutes can be used to manage your energy—to get up, walk around, do some arm circles, a quick meditation, a few burpees, and so forth—whatever you need to do to keep your energy up and stay in a peak state.

MONOTASKING: DAILY SCHEDULE

Here's a sample agenda to give you a visual idea of what I'm talking about:

- 6:30 a.m. to 6:50 a.m.—Short workout (burpees or yoga)
- 7:00 a.m. to 7:30 a.m.—Meditation and day planning
- 7:40 a.m. to 8:10 a.m.—Shower and breakfast
- 8:15 a.m. to 9:00 a.m.—Critical emails
- 9:10 a.m. to 10:00 a.m.—Abstract for conference speaking engagement

- 10:10 a.m. to 12:00 p.m.—Meetings and phone calls
- 12:10 p.m. to 1:00 p.m.—Lunch
- 1:10 p.m. to 2:00 p.m.—Proposal for prospective new client
- 2:10 p.m. to 3:00 p.m.—Strategy
- 3:10 p.m. to 4:15 p.m.—Meetings
- 4:30 p.m. to 5:15 p.m.—Email

I like to leave ten-minute gaps between most activities to give myself time to get up, walk around, stretch, get water, or go to the restroom.

When you block out your time, you control your agenda. Instead of the supporting actor in someone else's movie, you reclaim your schedule and you are the star of your show. Distractions are everywhere, but when you block time, you limit them and ultimately get more productive work done. I realize things will come up and block time will not always work, but it is better to have a plan for your life and each day than leave it up to circumstance.

EXAMINE YOUR INTENTION

For some of you reading this, the idea of not reading and responding to email the moment it comes in may make you feel uncomfortable. I get it. I felt that way, too.

Breaking any habit is tough, so before you get started, here's another tip—I suggest examining the intention behind your behavior and your need to answer everything immediately. You aren't an ER doctor, so there is no real reason for you to be on call.

Why do you feel like you need to be?

Maybe you need to feel important. Maybe you need to be the

smartest person in the room. Maybe you're a people pleaser and have a hard time saying no. Whatever the reason, it's your problem to solve, not theirs. Your desire to please others is deterring you from being intentional in your life and causing you to be a slave to everyone else's.

Examine the intention behind your actions to determine why you behave the way you do so you can let go and focus on yourself.

RECLAIM YOUR AGENDA

A true measure of intelligence is how you live your life, not how many things you can do at the same time. Doug had six different monitors, and he still couldn't accomplish anything that moved the needle for him or the company. He was constantly distracted trying to keep up with everything, but the irony was that he wasn't able to keep up with *anything*.

The trainers at New Skete Monastery teach their German shepherds how to focus, and they do an incredible job. When Itzler tried to distract Rainbow, it didn't matter what he did; nothing worked. She was laser-focused, and there was nothing in the world that was going to break her concentration.

As company leaders, we want our technical employees to be as focused as Rainbow. We don't want them distracted by email, instant messages, and unnecessary meetings; we don't want them context switching because it causes anxiety and a lack of productivity. We want them focused on one thing at a time because it improves their presence and the quality of their work. To do this, we need to steer them away from multitasking.

Multitasking is a hard habit to break, though, because we've all been brainwashed to believe it works. People brag about their multitasking skills on their résumés and LinkedIn profiles because more often than not, multitasking is rewarded. "Brian is such a fantastic multitasker. He gets so much done." The reality is, Brian is busy but not productive.

Multitasking in no longer in style, however. Today, deep focus is all the rage. Do you remember those bright *Miami Vice* suits that were popular in the eighties? Dressing like Sonny or Rico used to be in fashion, but if you wore one of those suits to the office today, people would probably raise an eyebrow. Multitasking is like those suits. It used to be cool, but today, it isn't. Today, it's all about *mono*tasking.

The best way to achieve your goals is to live your life on your own time. When you monotask, you reclaim your agenda.

You're also more productive. You'll get more done in one hour of monotasking than you will in fifteen hours of multitasking, and to win the cybersecurity war, we need all the help we can get.

We're almost at the end of the Secure Methodology, but we still have two more steps to go. Empathy is a people skill our technical employees need to have if we want to win the war, so let's talk about that next.

EXERCISE: DEVELOP MONOTASKING

Multitasking used to be all the rage, but today, the emphasis is on *mono*tasking. When I hire, I look for people who know how to focus, and I shy away from candidates who have "multitask" written on their résumés. The purpose of this exercise is to foster a culture of monotasking and focus.

Activity 1:
Block Time

In this activity, we're going to work with block time to create a daily schedule.

Overview: Dividing your day into time blocks will allow you to work on the things that matter the most, be in control of your time, and improve your productivity.

Objective: To develop more proactiveness, increased productivity, and movement on the things that matter most.

Preparation: Ask your team to bring a list of their professional goals for the year. If they don't have any, ask them to create some. These don't have to be SMART goals or anything sanctioned by HR—they can be *personal* professional goals. The specifics of the goals don't matter, just that there are some.

Materials: Pen and paper.

Step 1: Ask your team to write down the time they start their day at the top of a piece of paper and the time they end their day at the bottom.

Step 2: Ask them to think about the next day and to write in any meetings they have.

Step 3: Ask them to write in an hour for lunch.

Step 4: Ask them to pick an open hour for email. (Expect pushback on this, but be insistent. No one needs to spend more than an hour or two a day on email.)

Step 5: Ask them to pick an hour for short phone calls, instant messages, and text messages. (Again, no one needs to spend more than an hour a day doing all three of these things.)

Step 6: In the remaining time slots, ask them to refer to their goals and fill in relevant project work.

Step 7: Ask them to repeat this process every day for three weeks.

Step 8: At the end of the three weeks, call everyone together again to debrief. Did everyone accomplish more or less? What is the general feeling about the exercise? Who would continue the practice unprompted?

You'll find that most of your employees will prefer using block time to schedule their day because they feel less stressed and are able to get more done. Block time is a fantastic way to encourage monotasking and reclaim your agenda.

Activity 2:
Dream Killer or Enabler

Most of us have a big project we want to accomplish, such as writing a book, running a marathon, or learning a new skill. We often don't make the time for these projects, though, and they never move off the bucket list.

Overview: If you estimate the time these projects will take and then schedule them into your day, week, month, and year, you will either make steady progress or determine if it's something you aren't willing to dedicate the time to achieve.

Objective: To determine how many hours you need to accomplish a big project and to either schedule this time into your day/week/month/year to make it happen or remove it from your bucket list.

Preparation: Pick a long-term goal to focus on.

Materials: Pen and paper, calendar.

Step 1: Estimate how many hours it will take to accomplish the goal. You can use a **work-breakdown structure (WBS)** to help with this. First, identify the high-level tasks you need to complete and then how many hours it will take to finish each task.

Here is a quick example of a WBS:

Goal: Write a book

Tasks:

- **Idea:** 40 hours
- **Outline:** 40 hours
- **Content:** 320 hours (8 chapters at 40 hours per chapter)
- **Revisions:** 160 hours (8 chapters at 20 hours per chapter)
- **Editing and publishing:** 120 hours
- **Miscellaneous:** 80 hours
- **Total:** 760 hours

Step 2: How many hours can you spare each week to accomplish this goal?

Step 3: How many weeks will the project take to complete? (Divide the total number of hours needed to accomplish the goal by the number of hours you can spare each week.)

Step 4: Now that you know the full-time commitment required, is this goal something you still want to accomplish?

When we leave life to circumstance and only work on long-term goals in our "free time," accomplishing those goals takes a lot longer, if they're accomplished at all. Fully understanding the time commitment it takes to achieve our goals and then setting aside deliberate, intentional time to work on them helps us either accomplish our goals faster or decide not to pursue them at all.

CHAPTER 8

■ ■ ■

STEP 6: EMPATHY

The functions of intellect are insufficient without courage, love, friendship, compassion, and empathy.

—DEAN KOONTZ

A few years back, I was traveling back to St. Louis from a conference in Houston. I was walking through the airport with four other people, all technical, when I saw someone fall down. He was foaming at the mouth and having a seizure.

Immediately, I stopped to help and asked someone to contact airport security, but the four people I was with kept walking. Unlike me, they didn't stop to help.

When I caught up with them later, I said, "Why did you all just walk by like that? Why didn't you stop to help him?"

"Why should we have stopped?" they replied. "We didn't know what to do."

"Wouldn't you want someone to help you if you were having a seizure?"

It was like talking to a wall. These technical colleagues had no empathy or, like a lot of people, assumed someone else would step up to help this stranger, and there was nothing I was going to say to change that. A man was on the floor having a seizure, but because they didn't know what to do, they walked right by as if he didn't exist.

NLP PRESUPPOSITIONS FOR EMPATHY

- **People are not their behaviors.**
  (Accept the person; change the behavior.)
- **Everyone is doing the best they can with the resources they have available.**
  (Behavior is geared for adaptation, and present behavior is the best choice available. Every behavior is motivated by positive intent.)
- **People have all the resources they need to succeed and to achieve their desired outcomes.**
  (There are no unresourceful people, only unresourceful states.)

FOCUSED ON DIFFERENCES

Instead of helping and connecting with another human being to help a man having a seizure, my colleagues chose to ignore the problem. They had no empathy for a human being who was in medical need.

A lack of empathy is common among technical people, but I also think it's common among people in general. We all focus on the differences between us when we should be focusing on the similarities. When we do, we will naturally have more empathy for others.

US VERSUS THEM

We rarely focus on similarities, and the media and politics don't help. We are constantly bombarded with "us versus them" language:

- Rich versus poor
- Black versus white
- Democrat versus Republican
- COVID-19 mask supporter versus COVID-19 mask hater
- Pro-GMO versus anti-GMO

The list could go on and on. Focusing on similarities establishes common ground, builds rapport, and helps us work together better, but we rarely do it.

We all have common human experiences, such as financial problems and health issues. We all have struggles and challenges, good days and bad. We have days when we feel on top of the world and others when all we want to do is forget our troubles and watch twelve straight hours of Netflix.

We focus on the differences, though, and that keeps us apart. Focusing on differences deters empathy and encourages hatred in many cases.

This behavior is deeply embedded in our language. *He's an engineer. She's an executive.* Instead of calling them team members, we point out their differences. They could have something incredible in common, such as ultra-running or a favorite band or artist, but instead of categorizing them as *ultra-runners* or *Black Sabbath fans*, we classify them by their differences.

CHANGE THE WORLD

The main reason the Cold War ended between Russia and the United States (and why we avoided nuclear war) was because US President Ronald Reagan and USSR General Secretary Mikhail Gorbachev became friends. They didn't start off that way, but Reagan made the effort to see Gorbachev as a man no different than himself—he put himself in Gorbachev's shoes.[39] In his book *The Reagan Files*, author Jason Saltoun-Ebin writes:

"Perhaps then the real story of the end of the Cold War is just a simple tale of how an old hard-line anti-Communist President of the United States and a young Soviet reformer discovered that, despite their vast differences, all they needed to do was find one common area of agreement to change the world. The elimination of nuclear weapons became their focus."

This is no different than a common area of agreement on how to stop cybercriminals.

It's hard to achieve a common goal when no one agrees on the problem. In cybersecurity, this is heightened by a "techies" versus "management" mentality. We, as leaders, need to bridge the gap and remember what we ultimately want—to win the cyberwar and protect our data from enemies.

We do this externally, too. *She's a Microsoft person. He's an Apple guy.* The easiest way to create a divide is by the words and language we use. I refer to everyone on my team as team members,

---

39   Lesley Kennedy, "How Gorbachev and Reagan's Friendship Helped Thaw the Cold War," *History*, last modified October 24, 2019, https://www.history.com/news/gorbachev-reagan-cold-war#:~:text=President%20Ronald%20Reagan%20and%20Soviet,Forces%20Reduction%20Treaty%2C%20in%201987.

regardless of which department they work for. When everyone identifies with the same team, they naturally work together to get things done.

It's okay to have different functions and roles, but extensive labeling and stereotyping naturally reduces someone to a set of beliefs and diminishes the human element. When you use terms like "Karen is an engineer" or "Michael is a salesperson," you're essentially dehumanizing them. Karen is more than an engineer and Michael is more than a salesperson. Alternatively, it is better to say, "Karen's role in our organization is a cybersecurity engineer." These are subtle changes, yet the distinction is important.

Monitoring your language, especially when it comes to identity versus behavior, is paramount to interacting with your team. For instance, instead of telling someone they are "lazy," it is better to say they "act lazy." Saying "You are this" implies a label, which is tied to identity. A description of behavior such as, "You act lazy in this scenario," is much more effective. It may not seem like much of a difference to the person stating these things, but there's a *huge* difference to the person receiving them.

THE IMPACT ON CYBERSECURITY

Focusing on differences creates a divide. It also leads to some of the behavior we've been discussing throughout the book: intellectual bullying and egotism.

INTELLECTUAL BULLYING

Within the cybersecurity industry, a lack of empathy and "look the other way" culture has resulted in intellectual bullying by technical employees. I have noticed this is especially true of technical managers who love to bully down and kiss up. Their supervisors love them, but their employees sure don't. People like this keep other people down to lift themselves up. This behavior is often downplayed and considered "part of the culture," but that doesn't make it right. Ultimately, it's up to company leadership to define and enforce company culture, not technical employees.

Most of these bullies have been bullied themselves, so you would think they would naturally have more empathy, but the opposite is more often true. Instead, they put up walls as a defense mechanism and do the bullying before they can be bullied themselves.

TALL POPPY SYNDROME

When COVID-19 first hit, I spent a lot of time in Ireland. It was there that I first learned about tall poppy syndrome.

Tall poppy syndrome refers to someone who, in order to be the tallest poppy themselves, would rather chop down the tallest poppy in the field than celebrate it, or try to make themself taller through their own improvement. Tall poppy syndrome is about bringing other people down when they achieve something great. It's oppressive.

Tall poppy syndrome stems from insecurities. I dealt with this growing up, as my family used to say things like, "Do you think you're too good for us?" or "We're not all a Mr. Big Shot, like you." I had ambition, aspiration, and drive and was the first person in my family to graduate college, and they cut me down for it.

EGOTISM

A disproportionate ego cripples empathy. It's hard to be empathetic when you're only concerned about yourself. How can you be empathetic to someone else's challenges and struggles when all you care about is being the smartest person in the room? Egotism is self-consuming—that's the very nature of it.

Both bullying and egotism negatively impact the cybersecurity industry. When management talks down to their staff, it's less likely they will want to partner *with* management to solve problems. And as we've seen in previous chapters, effective communication is impossible if one person is too concerned with himself or herself to listen and understand someone else's challenges.

LACK OF EMPATHY WITH CLIENTS

Problems arise when we don't understand where our clients are coming from. We need to empathize with our clients and put ourselves in their shoes so we provide the best, most effective service. We need to be able to identify with them to better understand their needs, recognize the risks, and do a good job securing their data and systems.

So many cybersecurity people fail to take their clients' specific needs into consideration when developing strategies to secure their data and devices. This goes back to the overgeneralized and overly complicated frameworks I mentioned at the beginning of the book.

"To secure your data, you need to do all one hundred items on this checklist."

"I don't have the resources to do all of that. Tell me the most important things to do."

"You really need to do everything on this list if you want to secure your data."

For most technical people, it's all or nothing. They have a difficult time empathizing with a client's lack of resources, for example, so they can't come up with simple solutions. As a result, all one hundred items on their framework get done at 5 percent, and nothing is fully completed, least of all those Top 5 CIS Controls[40] I mentioned at the very beginning of the book.

Once again, this works to the cybercriminals' advantage. An understanding of risk and prioritization are critical to success in cybersecurity.

Please Keep Me in the Loop

Once, I sat in on a kickoff call with a new client, my COO, and Doug, who was assigned to the account (he still worked for Alpine Security back then). The new client, a new CISO, wanted us to do a cybersecurity assessment for his company, but he was nervous. He had never done one before and needed to report the results to his CEO.

"Please keep me in the loop. I have no idea what to expect, and I'm worried about it."

As the project progressed, I was shocked to learn Doug wasn't

---

40   Tim White, "Achieve Continuous Security and Compliance with the CIS Critical Security Controls," Qualys, September 26, 2017, https://blog.qualys.com/news/2017/09/26/achieve-continuous-security-and-compliance-with-the-cis-critical-security-controls.

keeping the CISO in the loop, which he had specifically requested. He was emailing the CISO weekly with updates per our company's standard operating procedure, yet this was only a two-week engagement. This client requested to be updated frequently and expressed nervousness about the testing, which should have been a clue to increase communication.

If Doug had been empathetic to the CISO's anxiety about running a cybersecurity assessment, he might have thought to send updates *daily*, not *weekly*. His lack of empathy had the potential to negatively impact the relationship with our client.

Fortunately, we caught this after a few days and asked Doug to send daily updates. We explained to him why this was important—that it is our job to provide value, make them secure, *and* give them a great experience. The great experience part is often what is missing because it requires people skills. Everyone wants to be understood and appreciated. Clients, too.

It's no different than avoiding restaurants with crappy service. The food may be top notch, but the overall experience will suffer if you have to deal with a rude server or dirty napkins.

LACK OF EMPATHY WITH COLLEAGUES

I've also seen struggles with empathy impact the internal team. A lot of people in my organization are often good at being empathetic with clients but struggle with empathy when they communicate internally. They know how to interact *externally*, but inside my company, there sometimes is a sense of "We're family. We don't have to be as empathetic."

Sometimes in business, we think we need to be empathetic only with clients or people we work with externally, but everyone we encounter is struggling with some kind of barrier.

I'm not good enough. I'm not smart enough. I'm not a logical thinker. I don't have this capability. I'm not a good reader.

We all have beliefs and misconceptions about ourselves that we believe limit our capabilities, so shouldn't we be empathetic with everyone we encounter?

Empathy allows us to recognize these beliefs, struggles, and limitations in our colleagues, coworkers, and direct reports. For management, it also allows us to discover what truly motivates our employees. If we know what they're motivated by, we may be able to leverage that motivation to help them overcome professional barriers.

When we aren't empathetic to our teammates' challenges, we create a divide, making it harder to work together. We also make it harder to communicate. If someone doesn't feel understood, it's unlikely they'll feel comfortable having open and honest conversations. If we want to defeat the bad guys, the good guys have to stick and work well together. A lack of empathy for your colleagues prevents that.

Team cohesion is important for effectiveness, a concept that is studied extensively in the military. Dr. Lauren Anderson and her team of professors conducted a study to learn about cohesion within military units and found it's achieved through bonding and empathy.[41] The more cohesion, the more effectiveness and better mental health for all involved.

THE HUMAN CONNECTION

Increasing empathy isn't easy and takes years to master. It takes change, which means embracing discomfort, something that is hard for me, too. To grow, I need to embrace empathy and the change and discomfort that come along with it. I know growth isn't only rainbows and unicorns, but I embody it anyway.

Throughout my years in cybersecurity, I discovered that in real life most technical employees struggle with empathy because they struggle with human connection. They don't like small talk, chitchat, or speaking in general. These employees tend to keep to themselves and focus all of their attention on their work or interests. You'll rarely find them in the break room socializing. The irony is, when I played World of Warcraft, we socialized in the game way more than we did in real life.

In order to be empathetic, both in business and in personal life, connecting with other humans is essential. In business, it allows us to better communicate with our colleagues and managers. In our personal lives, we communicate better with our friends and family. It can even help us connect with total strangers.

A couple of decades ago, I was in a tough spot. I had just gotten a divorce and was quite depressed, confused, and not in a good place. I was in line at the grocery store (my local Schnucks), and my state of mind must have been written all over my face because while I was checking out, the cashier looked me in the eye and said, "How are you doing?" She said this not in a small talk kind of way but with real concern.

---

41 Lauren Anderson, Laura Campbell-Sills, Robert J. Ursano, Ronald C. Kessler, Xiaoying Sun, Steven G. Heeringa, Matthew K. Nock, et al., "Prospective Associations of Perceived Unit Cohesion with Postdeployment Mental Health Outcomes," *Depression and Anxiety* 36 (2019): 511-21, https://nocklab.fas.harvard.edu/files/nocklab/files/anderson_et_al._2019.pdf.

At first, I was a little taken aback. Had this stranger really shown me compassion and caring in a time of need? I quickly realized she was showing me empathy, however, and was trying to connect with me. She could tell something was wrong and had the wherewithal to ask me whether or not I was okay. That moment and demonstration of kindness, albeit small, has stuck with me all these years because it highlighted the importance of the human connection.

I don't know why, but I still tear up some when I think about that moment. I felt alone, disconnected, and depressed, yet that simple gesture made me realize I wasn't alone and that strangers care.

SMALL GESTURES

When talking about the human connection, something small can make a massive difference. We often dismiss and overlook how important the small gestures are because many of us believe an act of kindness needs to be miraculous to have an impact, like the gift of a new car. Sometimes a friendly smile or simple question is all it takes to have a meaningful connection. We're all on this planet together. What's wrong with being nice to others and connecting?

Tony Robbins has a similar, defining story. He grew up poor, and his family often had no money to spend on Thanksgiving dinner. His father was a proud man and stubborn. He was bitter he couldn't afford to give his family a turkey dinner for the holiday but was too obstinate to accept any help from anyone.

One year, that all changed. A stranger knew that Robbins and his family were struggling, so he stopped by the house with a bag of groceries. Robbins remembers his father refusing the help as he tried to push the stranger away, but the stranger was persistent. He stuck his foot in the door to hold it open and said, "It's okay, sir. Your family deserves some food. I know you're struggling."

It was at this point Robbins realized that strangers care. It was a defining moment for him, and he discovered he wanted to help other people as well. In the grand scheme of things, buying a family a bag of groceries for Thanksgiving is a somewhat small gesture, but it changed the entire trajectory of Robbins's life. Empathy, compassion, and the human connection have the power to do that.

TWO CATEGORIES OF EMPATHY

Did you know there are two different categories of empathy?

Most of the people I talk to about empathy and the Secure Methodology don't. They think there is only one form of empathy, the emotional kind.

However, there are two different categories of empathy. There is **affective empathy** and **cognitive empathy.**

This diagram shows different styles of leadership and why it's best to avoid the low/low and the high/high. I personally think the *high cognitive* and *low affective* is the best for a leader in cybersecurity and is how I lead. I have found the friendly colleague leader is ineffective.

Affective empathy (also known as emotional empathy) is the empathy we all think about first. If someone is in pain and you feel the pain, too, you are being emotionally empathetic. Although this book advocates for cognitive empathy (understanding with our heads), affective empathy (feeling with our heart) can serve a purpose as well when dealing with a friend or family member.

Cognitive empathy is different. It's the ability to understand *someone else's* feelings and see things from their perspective. Cognitive empathy is logical and can help us better understand other people and their motivations. When we talk about improving our technical team's empathy, we're talking about their *cognitive* empathy. That's the type of empathy we want to focus on.

TIPS AND TRICKS: DEVELOP COGNITIVE EMPATHY

We want our technical employees to be cognitively empathetic. We want them to understand the feelings of their clients and colleagues so they can communicate effectively and work well with others to solve problems.

Teaching your technical staff cognitive empathy is tough, but there are a few tips you can try.

Motivation

Think back to the Secure Methodology step on mindset. To teach your team how to be more empathetic, you need to first understand what motivates them.

Why are they pursuing a career in cybersecurity in the first place? If it's to help protect sensitive data, reminding them of this may help with their cognitive empathy.

If your team understands their why and how they fit into the big picture, they will be more likely to see themselves as a unit working toward something together, rather than as individuals. If we are motivated to accomplish something, we are more likely to take the steps to figure it out.

Doug was (and still probably is) only motivated by being the smartest person in the room. This trumped everything and motivated all of his behavior.

Acknowledgment

If you want your technical employees to be empathetic, you also must acknowledge their accomplishments. Highly technical people worked hard for their skills and often feel underappreciated. If you recognize that hard work, they will feel more connected to you and will be more likely to improve their cognitive empathy.

You also want to acknowledge your technical team's similarities, struggles, and perspectives, as well as the efforts they've made to enhance their own empathy. If they haven't practiced empathy in the past, learning it can be a challenge, so a little acknowledgment for small gains is good and will encourage further growth.

Adapt Your Communication

This is a tip for leadership—you need to be as cognitively empathetic with your technical team as you expect them to be with clients and each other. In this case, you need to be empathetic with the difficulties of the industry.

Many technical people struggle with admitting when something is tough. They have a hard time asking for help. This results in issues because it causes miscommunication around deadlines. If the technical team doesn't know how long something will take because they don't fully understand the problem, how can leadership set deadlines?

Be empathetic to this struggle by adapting your communication with your team. Instead of asking questions, try statements. Remember to avoid asking why questions (or why statements) because they typically put people on the defensive. Avoid the word *why*, and you'll be fine.

*Tell me **what** you know.*

*Tell me **how** you're going to plan to do this.*

If there isn't a plan, you know the team needs time to figure that out. This will help you plan for that extra time, which positively impacts everyone.

Your technical team meets their deadlines with you, and you meet your deadlines with your board. It's win-win.

As a leader, never assume something in cybersecurity is going to be easy because it almost never is. It is often simple but rarely easy.

SIX-PHASE GUIDED MEDITATION

The Six-Phase Guided Meditation practice by Vishen Lakhiani is another tool you can use to help develop your technical staff's cognitive empathy. You can find it on YouTube[42] or the Omvana[43] app.

It's an active "creative visualization" meditation practice, which goes against the grain. Typically, in meditation, we're trying to clear our minds and think of nothing in order to train specific brainwaves or achieve an altered state of consciousness. Six-Phase Guided Meditation isn't that—it's an active visualization and creative imagination practice, sort of like daydreaming but with intention. I recommend you start practicing this meditation and, if you like it, introduce it to your technical team. This will increase their empathy and awareness.

This meditation practice is creative visualization. I recommend listening to and practicing the meditation in full so you thoroughly understand and benefit from it. The entire session is roughly twenty minutes, which may seem like a long time for some, but for reference, fourteen minutes is less than 1 percent of our day.

---

42 Vishen Lakhiani, "The 6 Phase Meditation," YouTube, February 13, 2013, https://www.youtube.com/watch?v=EaRu14P9H84.

43 Omvana (website), https://www.omvana.com/.

Here are the benefits of the six phases.

Phase One—Connection

Benefit: Most of us have a considerable disconnection to people in our own families and workplace. By thinking about their own consciousness and how it interacts with the world around them, your team will naturally think about the world from the perspective of others.

Phase Two—Gratitude

Benefit: Gratitude makes us think about what we have, rather than what we want. When your team is grateful, they will be more empathetic to the struggles of others because they won't be preoccupied with struggles of their own.

Phase Three—Release Negative Charges

Benefit: The grudges and judgments we hold toward others carry significant energetic charges that alter our mood, health, and feelings in a negative manner. When your team puts themselves in the shoes of people they've had confrontations with, it will be easier for them to put themselves in the shoes of their coworkers and clients as well.

Phase Four—Visualize Your Perfect Future

Benefit: We rarely make space to think about what we really want in life or what our perfect life would look like—it's hard to live a perfect life when you've never thought about it. By thinking about their perfect, ideal life, your technical team will create a target to strive toward.

Phase Five—Intentions

Benefit: Many of us are victims of circumstance and allow things to hold us back or alter our mood. Your technical team can use this phase to set their intentions for the day, which will help them to take control of their lives and enhance their moods.

Phase Six—The Blessing

Benefit: We are all supported in both seen and unseen ways, in ways we understand and in ways we don't. This phase will help your technical team see that support is all around them—their family, their team, their leadership, nature, or even the strength inside themselves.

I highly recommended the Six-Phase Guided Meditation for everyone in your organization, not just your technical employees. I also recommend the Calm app (alternating between the two is what works best for me). Positive visualization is important because it helps us achieve our goals. When we cultivate gratitude and let go of our tension, we improve our mindset and strengthen empathy.

YOU AREN'T ALONE

Do you remember the story I told you about checking out at Schnucks? Even though I felt alone and disconnected, I wasn't—someone (the warm and friendly cashier) offered support. These small gestures happen all the time, yet we are typically unaware of them, simply because we aren't in tune with our surroundings. Meditation helps with that, which is why I do it consistently.

EMPHASIZE SIMILARITIES

I wasn't naturally cognitively empathetic when I first started my company. It was something I had to develop over time, and I am still developing it today. I used to think everyone should be like me—that things that took me an hour should take other people an hour to do as well. Back in the day, I was focused on being the smartest person in the room.

A lack of cognitive empathy isn't just something technical employees struggle with, like my colleagues in the Houston airport. (I still can't believe they didn't stop to help that guy.) It can be found at all levels and within all departments of any organization, so don't assume someone you're working with is cognitively empathetic, even if it's the CEO. Don't take it for granted.

The words we use have the power to divide us. We struggle with cognitive empathy because we emphasize differences when we should emphasize similarities. When it's absent, intellectual bullying and egotism kick in, impacting our ability to communicate and work together to solve problems.

We need cognitive empathy to defeat cybercriminals and win the war. We need to connect with our clients so we can see the problem from their perspective and provide solutions that will help them achieve their goals, reduce risk, and become more secure. We need to connect with our internal team to communicate effectively and work together to problem solve.

Once we have all the steps in the Secure Methodology down—awareness, mindset, acknowledgment, communication, monotasking, and empathy—we move into the seventh and final step, kaizen. Let's get into it now.

EXERCISE: AWAKEN COGNITIVE EMPATHY

When they hear the word *empathy*, most people think of affective (emotional) empathy rather than cognitive empathy. Although affective empathy is rarely useful in business, *cognitive* empathy always is. These two activities will help you and your team awaken cognitive empathy.

Activity 1:
Assumptions and Similarities

Overview: We often make erroneous assumptions about others and ignore similarities. Finding things in common builds rapport and helps us develop cognitive empathy because we realize we are more similar than we initially thought.

Objective: To build rapport, understanding, and cognitive empathy with your colleagues.

Preparation: For this exercise, you want your team to work with partners; however, it's critical the partners don't work together directly or know each other well. This may require you to pair your team up ahead of time.

Materials: Pen and paper.

Step 1: Pair your team up in partners of two, following the instructions above.

Step 2: Using the materials, ask each person to describe their partner based only on assumptions. These could be assumptions based on what they wear, how they talk, or what their job is. (Make sure to tell your team to keep the assumptions positive.)

Step 3: Have each partner share and make note of any assumptions they got right. Flip a coin to determine who goes first.

Step 4: Next, ask the pairs to find something they have in common. It can be anything—it can be a hobby, a favorite food, or a travel destination. It can even be a preference for blue ink over black. It doesn't matter what it is, just that they find *something* in common. If they have a hard time, they can ask you for some help.

Step 5: Ask each pair to share what they have in common. You'd be surprised by how many others chime in when they have something in common with the sharers, too.

This activity will help your technical team to stop making assumptions and start looking for similarities, which will help develop their empathy.

Activity 2:
The Bully's Shoes

Overview: Bullies have their own struggles, were often bullied them-selves, and often just want to be appreciated. When we see things from their perspective, we can empathize with them and improve our understanding.

Objective: To see the world from the perspective of bullies and develop cognitive empathy and better skills to improve interactions with them.

Preparation: You want your team to work with partners for this exercise. To save time, consider pairing them up ahead of time. Matching employ-ees with varying backgrounds will increase insights. You also want to make copies of the NLP Presuppositions for Empathy listed earlier in the chapter. Here they are again for quick reference:

- People are not their behaviors.
- Everyone is doing the best they can with the resources they have available. (Behavior is geared for adaptation, and present behavior

is the best choice available. Every behavior is motivated by positive intent.)

- People have all the resources they need to succeed and to achieve their desired outcomes. (There are no unresourceful people, only unresourceful states.)

Materials: Pen and paper, copies of the NLP Presuppositions for Empathy.

Step 1: Schedule a meeting and tell your team ahead of time what to expect.

Step 2: At the beginning of the meeting, pair employees up and pass out the NLP Presuppositions for Empathy copies.

Step 3: Ask your team to each think of a bully. This could be someone inside or outside the organization.

Step 4: Have partner A describe the bully and what they do that makes them one.

Step 5: Next, have them put themselves in their bully's shoes. Have partner A run through each of the three NLP presuppositions listed on the handout and apply them to the bully as a point of discussion and means for cognitive empathy.

- What is really going on with them?
- What was their childhood like?
- What is it like to be them on a daily basis?
- What insecurities are they dealing with?

Step 6: Finally, ask partner A to identify anything they can do to alter their approach dealing with this person in the future.

Step 7: Ask the partners to switch. Partner B now repeats steps 4 through 6.

Working in partners allows your team to get additional perspectives on the different types of bullies and come up with joint solutions on ways to best deal with the bully.

CHAPTER 9

✳ ✳ ✳

STEP 7: KAIZEN

Excellent firms don't believe in excellence—only in constant improvement and constant change.

—TOM PETERS

At the beginning of 2020, I made plans to visit Dublin, Ireland, in the middle of March. I was booked to stay there for ten days.

Then, at the beginning of March, COVID-19 started to spread rapidly in the United States. The number of reported cases in New York and Washington State were increasing, and more and more pockets of cases were popping up in other states, too. The situation wasn't looking good.

In many places in Europe, the situation was even much worse, and several regions of the continent were already shut down. I decided to take my outbound flight to Dublin anyway.

Shortly after I arrived, the US government announced it would be restricting travel to and from Europe to contain the outbreak. The last flight to Saint Louis was to depart from the Dublin airport twenty-four hours after I arrived.

Most of the people I talked to assumed I would board the return flight and head back home, but I didn't. Instead, I decided to stay in Dublin indefinitely.

I think this was easy for me because I am comfortable with being uncomfortable. I don't seek uncertainty in a carefree way; I assess the risk and then make my decision. Choosing to stay in Ireland was no different. I knew the possibility of getting stuck in Ireland was high, but I examined all the risks and decided it was worth it.

NLP PRESUPPOSITIONS FOR KAIZEN

- **There is ONLY feedback!**
  (There is no failure, only feedback.)
- **Everyone is doing the best they can with the resources they have available.**
  (Behavior is geared for adaptation, and present behavior is the best choice available. Every behavior is motivated by a positive intent.)
- **All procedures should increase wholeness.**
- **All procedures should be designed to increase choice.**

WHAT IS KAIZEN?

I decided to stay in Dublin and embrace the uncertainty. Life is a journey, full of twists and turns, and uncertainty is the *only* thing we can be certain of. That's why I choose to be flexible and adaptable—so I can handle those twists and turns with ease.

Like life, the Secure Methodology is a journey. It isn't a silver bullet, and it isn't going to improve the people skills of your technical staff or make us victorious in the cybersecurity war overnight. It takes time and consistent effort.

Kaizen is a Japanese business philosophy and means "continuous improvement." Kaizen (改善) is the Sino-Japanese word for "improvement." Once you have a process or procedure in place, kaizen is the act of continuously looking for ways to improve it. For example, if you have a specific communication practice for interacting with your clients, tweaking and fine-tuning that communication practice to get a better response would be kaizen.

One of the key aspects of kaizen is that it gives you permission to start and then continuously improve. Too many people try to make everything perfect before they start something new, such as working on this methodology or trying a new cybersecurity countermeasure. The reality is that perfection is the enemy of execution.

Constant and never-ending improvement (CANI) is another way to say kaizen and may be easier for some of you and your technical team to understand (the term *kaizen* is pretty cool, though). When you try something new, you aren't going to get it right the first or even second time around. You're going to have to practice achieving the results you want. True mastery will take a lifetime of improvement and refinement because it is an uncertain journey. The focus must be on the outcome, not the obstacles.

ROOT CAUSE ANALYSIS

This step in the Secure Methodology isn't an in-depth discussion of kaizen but an acceptance of the kaizen philosophy with an emphasis on **root cause analysis** and continuous improvement. Root cause analysis helps us understand the real problem, which is needed in order to improve.

The 5 Whys is a great root cause analysis exercise. This is different than the 7 Levels Deep Exercise used in the Mindset step to help you and your team discover your why. The 5 Whys is used to get to the true source of a problem so improvement can be made and kaizen practiced.

Here is an example in action:

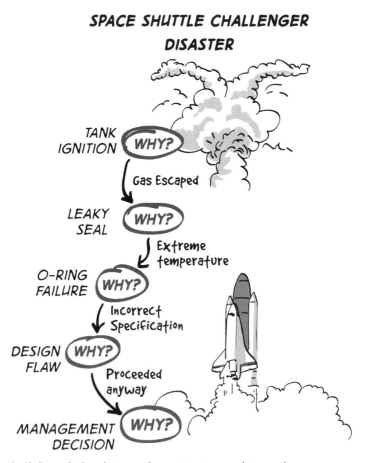

SPACE SHUTTLE CHALLENGER DISASTER

TANK IGNITION — WHY?

Gas Escaped

LEAKY SEAL — WHY?

Extreme temperature

O-RING FAILURE — WHY?

Incorrect Specification

DESIGN FLAW — WHY?

Proceeded anyway

MANAGEMENT DECISION — WHY?

The *Challenger* shuttle explosion provides a great root cause analysis example.

In this diagram, we start at the top and ask:

Why did the *Challenger* blow up?

There was a tank ignition.

Why was there a tank ignition?

There was escaping gas caused by a leaky seal.

Why was there a leaky seal?

There was extreme temperature caused by an O-ring failure.

Why was there an O-ring failure?

The specification was wrong due to a design flaw.

Why was there a design flaw?

Management decided to proceed anyway.

Also, it doesn't have to be five whys—you may need six or seven. What's important is getting to the root cause of the problem so you can make improvements and move forward. This concept applies to everything, including cybersecurity defenses and the Secure Methodology. If one of the steps isn't working for you and your team (for the life of you, you can't get your technical staff to stop multitasking), go through this exercise as a way to find out why.

THE FOUR PHASES OF KAIZEN

There are four phases of kaizen, and they apply to *everything* in life.

- Phase 1: *Identify* ways to improve
- Phase 2: *Plan* how to make those improvements
- Phase 3: *Execute* on the plan
- Phase 4: *Review* the effectiveness of the plan

Take a look at this chart for a visual description.

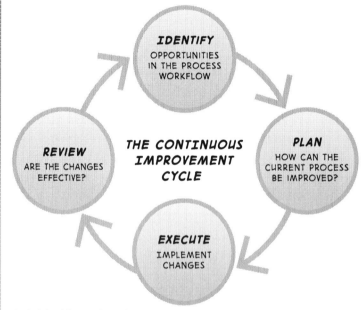

This high-level diagram depicts kaizen's main steps.

If you're trying to lose weight, you first **identify** an opportunity to lose weight (New Year's resolution), **plan** how to lose it (diet and exercise), **execute** the plan (switch to a healthy smoothie for breakfast and walk an hour a day), and then **review** the results (did you lose weight?).

Then, based on those results, you adjust the plan. If you didn't lose enough weight, you further modify your diet and increase your exercise. If you lost more weight than intended, scale those walks back or ditch the smoothie. The point is to keep repeating the process until you achieve the results you want.

NOTHING IS CERTAIN, EXCEPT UNCERTAINTY

Nothing is certain. The COVID-19 global pandemic taught us all that.

When you think about it, what *is* certain? The only thing *certain* is *un*certainty. Even the Secure Methodology is uncertain because different people will have a different response to it. Paradoxical as it is, uncertainty is the only thing we can all rely on.

We've been conditioned to think we have certainty, though. Just yesterday I was speaking to someone on my team—his 46-year-old uncle just died. He had a seizure, fell in the kitchen, and hit his head on the counter. As you can imagine, this came as a big shock to my team member and to his family.

It doesn't matter what we do today—each and every one of us may not make it to tomorrow. I have healthy friends who have died from a sudden heart attack. If you are a vegan and have a plant-based diet, it doesn't guarantee you'll live longer than everyone else. Life simply isn't that certain.

COVID-19 exposed the false sense of security we've all been feeling for decades, and most of us are freaking out because of it. In order to win the cybersecurity war *and* the internal war, however, we have to embrace uncertainty and discomfort. And we have to be okay with that discomfort in order to grow and improve. To achieve kaizen, we have to be adaptable.

Uncertainty along the journey is okay as long as we're learning and trying to make improvements. That is the nature of kaizen. It's even okay to take detours sometimes—at least you now know that is not the right path. Take Thomas Edison's advice: he "failed" at inventing the light bulb over 1,000 times, but he practiced kaizen.

I have gotten lots of results! I know several thousand things that won't work!

—THOMAS EDISON

WHEN IS THE PERFECT TIME TO START?

Many people decide they'll start when "things are right." These people will probably say the same thing about starting this methodology—they'll start when they have time, when it feels right, when it's the new year, and so on.

Why not start now? If you keep telling yourself you'll start something later, when "the planets are aligned" the reality is, you'll never do it.

This is where kaizen can help. Just start. Take the first step and work continuously to improve it. That's how I was able to write and publish this book.

TWO TYPES OF PEOPLE

There are two types of people in this world: **dabblers** and **masters**. To achieve kaizen, you have to be a master. Mastery is an endless pursuit.

Dabblers read something once and think they understand it. If they try something new and it doesn't work the way they thought it would, they give up. "That didn't work for me" is something you'll hear a dabbler say often. They have a fixed mindset. Doug is a dabbler.

Masters know true proficiency takes time. Improvement is a part of the process, so they expect uncertainty along the journey. Masters are flexible, adaptable, and open to change and trying new things. They embrace the growth mindset.

This graph is a good example of the master's journey.

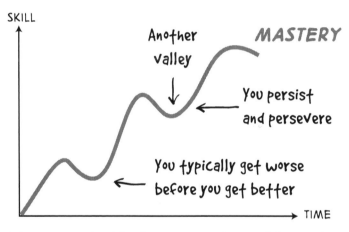

The key is to persevere through the valley—sometimes you will get worse before you get better. You may have to "unlearn" things you learned, especially when it comes to cybersecurity and people skills.

Because it is the process of never-ending improvement, achieving kaizen demands flexibility, reflection, root cause analysis, and adaptability. These qualities are a requirement.

Even Tiger Woods, one of the greatest golfers of all time, practices kaizen—he works constantly (and consistently) to improve his swing.

> *Because my chipping motion is tied to my full swing, it has changed as I've worked with different instructors over the years. At one point, I held the shaft more vertical and used a weaker grip. Then I switched up and my hands were lower at address than they are now. For me, getting comfortable with a new chipping motion has always been one of the hardest parts of a swing change, but it's vital.*[44]
>
> —TIGER WOODS

THE IMPACT ON CYBERSECURITY

We could say cybercriminals are kaizen masters—they're constantly changing and adapting to the controls that cybersecurity personnel put in place. The cybersecurity industry will suffer if we don't adopt the flexibility and adaptability of kaizen. To keep up with the cybercriminals, we need to measure the effectiveness of our efforts—when they aren't effective, we need to improve them. Isn't that how any business works? Without kaizen, our processes won't improve.

Right now, the industry needs more kaizen. If you don't believe me, take a look around. Does it look like we're winning? Every other day, email servers are being hacked and sensitive data is being stolen. This continues to happen because cybersecurity companies are still selling overcomplicated frameworks and checklists, and technical leaders are still buying them.

One root cause: many want a magic solution—new firewall, a next-gen appliance with AI, or some other silver bullet. Another is that most continue to hire paper tigers and other technical employees who struggle with people skills. We all talk about

---

44   Tiger Woods, "Here's How Tiger Woods Keeps Improving His Elite Short-Game," *Golf Digest*, April 2, 2020, https://www.golfdigest.com/story/heres-how-tiger-woods-keeps-improving-his-elite-short-game.

improving the technology, but as you've learned throughout this book, it's not about the technology—it's about the people. Who cares about the device if we don't have the right people in place to use it?

We need to apply the principles of kaizen to our technical team's people skills. We need to teach them the practices and processes to improve their skills, and then work continuously to refine them. When it comes to the cybersecurity war, we can't guess and hope for solutions. We have to be bold, take steps, improve, take additional steps, and improve again.

THE WASHINGTON MONUMENT

To practice kaizen and continuously improve, you need to first do a thorough root cause analysis of the entire problem. Here is an example of root cause analysis used to solve a problem with the Washington Monument.

- **Problem:** The Washington Monument is deteriorating.
- **Why #1:** Why is the monument deteriorating? Because harsh chemicals are frequently used to clean the monument.
- **Why #2:** Why are harsh chemicals used? To effectively clean off the large number of bird droppings on the monument.
- **Why #3:** Why are there a large number of bird droppings on the monument? Because the large population of spiders in and around the monument are a food source for local birds.
- **Why #4:** Why is there a large population of spiders in and around the monument? Because vast swarms of insects on which the spiders feed are drawn to the monument at dusk.
- **Why #5:** Why are swarms of insects drawn to the monument at dusk? Because the lighting of the monument in the evening attracts the local insects.

- **Solution:** Change how the monument is illuminated in the evening to prevent attraction of swarming insects.[45]

If whoever was trying to solve this problem stopped at the first why, the type of chemical being used to clean the monument likely would have been changed. That isn't the real issue, though. The real issue is the lights. Deep, thorough root cause analysis is a key element of kaizen.

ADAPTABILITY

To beat the bad guys, our technical team needs to practice kaizen. To practice kaizen, they have to be adaptable.

When I decided to stay in Dublin, I had to find an office space. My accommodations were terrific—and extremely comfortable—but the internet connection wasn't fast enough. I needed the capability to have video calls with my team back in Saint Louis, prospects, and clients, which required a fair amount of bandwidth. The place where I was staying, on the outskirts of town, simply didn't have a fast enough connection.

I had a few options and chose the one with the best internet connection. It was a wellness/yoga studio within a short drive of where I was staying, so it was an easy and convenient fix.

The only problem was that the wellness studio was also a sacred meditation space—I wasn't allowed to eat anything inside. The owner said the smell of the food would disrupt the energy of the studio, so if I wanted to eat, I would have to do it outside.

That would have been fine except that it was the middle of a

---

45 Alpine Security, "5 Whys Cause Analysis," YouTube, April 8, 2019, https://www.youtube.com/watch?v=1bkSO3Dupf8.

pandemic. Nothing was open for dine-in. Only takeaway was available. If I wanted to eat while I was at the office, I had to eat it outside, standing up, and in the rain—it rains nearly every day in Ireland.

Needless to say, that didn't last. I found a solution to my problem because my initial solution needed improvement. So I ditched the wellness studio and rented a studio apartment downtown at COVID-19 prices—around $60 a night. Normally, the place would be around $350 a night. I had high-speed internet, a kitchen (with a refrigerator), desk, sofa, bed, and shower. I first upgraded my "home office" with the wellness studio rental, and now I had upgraded it again. I had practiced kaizen, or continuous improvement.

This is just an example and highlights that the key is often just to start, like I did with the wellness studio. Once you start, you have a baseline to figure out what didn't work so you can make improvements or at least head in the right direction.

THE BIG LEAP

I recently listened to *The Big Leap* by Gay Hendricks, and this passage struck me in particular:

> *Each of us has an inner thermostat setting that determines how much love, success, and creativity we allow ourselves to enjoy. When we exceed our inner thermostat setting, we will often do something to sabotage ourselves, causing us to drop back into the old, familiar zone where we feel secure.*

I have a problem with my inner thermostat. I'm aware of it, yet it takes me a lot of effort to change it. When I'm on the verge of a breakthrough or improvement in something, I catch myself engaging in self-sabotage. It's as if my unconscious is telling me I need to get back to where I'm comfortable, so it creates a scenario that blocks the breakthrough of improvement.

This happens in all aspects of life when you're trying to learn something new. This is why the improvement curve for mastery has those valleys where you get worse before you get better. Everyone working on self-improvement (including your technical team) has to recognize this and push through it. This is one of the ways to win the internal war.

FEAR OF FAILURE

So many of us avoid doing something unfamiliar because we lack confidence and are afraid of failure. Either that or we can't stand the discomfort of stepping outside our comfort zone to try something new. I was in an unfamiliar and uncomfortable setting not once but *twice* when I was in Dublin. If I hadn't been adaptable, flexible, and determined to practice kaizen, I wouldn't have been able to be productive and get work done.

If you ignore the discomfort, you're never going to develop the skills you need to deal with rapidly changing situations. You have to welcome discomfort as an opportunity to be flexible and as an opportunity for growth. Remember the fixed versus growth mindset? You want the growth mindset.

Before COVID-19, we were all living very specific lifestyles. The coronavirus threw a wrench right smack in the middle of them and shattered our collective false sense of security. Overnight, everything became hectic and uncertain, and because we've all been so comfortable living with this false certainty for so long, we've forgotten how to adapt.

Regardless of COVID-19 (or anything else unpredictable that has the potential to throw life completely off its hinges), there is no certainty other than the certainty we create for ourselves. Everything else is just a bad habit that isn't serving us.

Relationships are a good example of this. People stay in relationships that aren't serving them because they're comfortable. They may not be happy or fulfilled, but they know exactly how things are going to work. They're afraid to leave because they're afraid of trying anything new. If they were adaptable, they may be able to make changes and find a new relationship. The same concept applies to anything—we often prefer the "devil we know," but improvement is often on the other side of discomfort we work so hard to avoid.

Kaizen requires adaptability. It requires examining what you currently have in place, finding the root cause of what needs to be improved, and making changes. If the change doesn't make improvements, you'll know what *doesn't* work, just as Edison did almost one thousand times before discovering the light bulb. If you aren't adaptable, you can't make changes, meaning you can't improve. Adaptability and kaizen go hand in hand.

BABY STEPS

Babies are incredibly adaptable and are in a perpetual state of kaizen, constantly looking to improve their existing processes. We often forget we were once babies, unafraid and full of wonder.

When a baby first starts to walk, for example, it will take a wobbly step or two before it falls down. Typically, the baby will get right back up and try another couple of steps only to fall down again. This continues on until the baby can walk across the room and down the hallway, and before you know it, you're chasing the now superspeedy baby all over the house.

When a baby falls down, it is learning how to balance. It gets back up in order to learn from the mistake of falling because the baby is motivated to improve and walk a few more steps. Falling is a part of the learning-to-walk process.

Can you imagine if a baby tried to take a couple of steps, fell down, and then never got back up? If the baby quit as soon as things got tough, it would never learn to walk. If it settled for a few good steps but then never tried for anything more, it wouldn't learn to walk either. Everything takes time to learn and then master, even walking. As babies, we did not get discouraged or say "Walking isn't for me"—we kept trying until we mastered walking and become unconsciously competent at it. All of us were born with a growth mindset, yet somewhere along the way, we lost it. We were told our limitations and we believed it.

We often forget this because we take these now innate skills for granted, but it took time to learn how to brush your teeth and tie your shoes, so why wouldn't it take time to learn how to improve your people skills? If your technical people give up as soon as they start to feel uncomfortable, they will never learn to improve their people skills, and the cybersecurity industry will continue to lose the war.

We were all born with an innate ability to deal with uncertainty, but it has been beaten out of us. We've been brainwashed to believe that we need to get something right on the first or second try, and when we don't, most of us quit. If we had to learn how to walk *now* as an adult, most of us probably wouldn't. Yet, it is with baby steps, one after the other, that we go the farthest.

MOTIVATION

A baby will continue to try to walk, even though it has fallen down time and time again because it is intrinsically motivated to walk. Walking, for a baby, is perceived as a necessity.

This is true for most humans—they are motivated by necessity. Most people don't act until their back is up against a wall. Motivation is what gets us started, habit keeps us going, and kaizen is what will help us reach our targets.

To encourage your technical team to implement kaizen and really improve and strengthen their people skills, you need to discover what motivates them. It may be the same motivation that got them in the right headspace in the Mindset step, but it may also be something different.

If you find your team is lacking the motivation to practice kaizen and continuously work on improving their people skills, I suggest revisiting the 7 Levels Deep activity in chapter 4. It will help you drill down and discover what motivates your team.

TIPS AND TRICKS: HIGH-PERFORMANCE HABITS

Brendon Burchard's book, *High Performance Habits*, talks about the following six high-performance habits (HP6), broken down into two categories:

Personal

1. Seek Clarity

2. Generate Energy

3. Raise Necessity

Social

4. Increase Productivity

5. Develop Influence

6. Demonstrate Courage

I've read this book multiple times and personally use Burchard's High-Performance Planner. Necessity is key, and we want to "raise" it. Then we act with intention and get things done in a timely manner, rather than waiting until it really is necessary and our back is against the wall.

The HP6 speaks nearly to everything we've covered in the book and is a simple way to monitor your improvement, also known as kaizen.

EMBRACE UNCERTAINTY

To defeat cybercriminals and win the war, our technical employees need to be adaptable, embrace uncertainty, and pursue never-ending improvement—they need to practice kaizen.

Many technical employees shy away from uncertainty in social situations, but when it comes to cybersecurity, they often deal with uncertainty. The uncertainty is technical, though, and dealing with it is a lot different.

A computer, for example, will respond the same way 99.9 percent of the time, so making adjustments and improvements is easier than with people. Humans are more likely to answer something *differently* 99.9 percent of the time, which is where the challenges your technical staff have often come into play.

If you ask one hundred computers a question, they'll give you the same answer every time. If you ask one hundred people a question, you'll almost get one hundred different answers. This uncertainty makes improvement with humans more challenging.

The only way to get better at something is to try it and practice it—to figure out what didn't work and make improvements. If you give up, you'll never learn to walk.

The Secure Methodology is a journey. It isn't a silver bullet and it isn't a "one and done"—it's a process centered on continuous improvement. Without kaizen, it doesn't work.

Uncertainty is one of the six human needs, and it shouldn't stop you from practicing the steps outlined in this methodology. We live with uncertainty daily, even without COVID-19. Regardless of how healthy we are, there is no guarantee that we'll be here tomorrow or that our life will be the same one day to the next. We could get a phone call that changes everything.

Nothing is certain, not even beliefs. People "discover" their spirituality all the time. The *only* thing certain is *un*certainty, so don't be afraid of it. Mastery is a journey (full of uncertain twists and turns), but if you practice kaizen, you can embrace that uncertainty to make improvements, and that's how you'll stay a step ahead of the cybercriminals and win the war.

Now that we've concluded the last step of the Secure Methodology, what's next? Growth and contribution.

EXERCISE: AMPLIFY KAIZEN

Kaizen means constant improvement. It's about establishing best practices and processes and then working continuously to make them better.

Activity 1:
Reflection Journal

Overview: Kaizen focuses on reflection and never-ending growth, so in this activity, you're going to ask your team to keep a workday reflection journal. Reflecting on each day's challenges and wins schedules time for you to find gratitude and ways to improve.

Objective: To schedule time, reflect, and find ways to overcome challenges, repeat wins, and appreciate the continuous improvement journey.

Preparation: Tell your technical team ahead of time what they're getting into—you don't want to catch them off-guard with something that's going to take an extra fifteen to twenty minutes of their day. Manage their expectations by telling them exactly what to anticipate. Some will still be opposed to the exercise, but you'll save yourself a lot of trouble if you give them a heads-up.

Materials: Pens, composition notebooks to use as journals

Step 1: Send the email letting your team know what the activity is (workday reflection journal) and how you expect them to interact. Be specific.

Step 2: Have a meeting to go over the basics of the activity and your expectations.

Step 3: Distribute the journals.

Step 4: In the journal, ask them to describe one challenge or one win each workday. Regardless of which they pick (challenge or win), they have to explain their reasons why and what they will do to either prevent it from happening again or repeat it in the future.

Step 5: Schedule one-on-one meetings with your team to go over their journals. Did they notice any patterns? What are their strengths and weaknesses? Where can processes be improved?

Step 6: During the one-on-one, create goals based on insights drawn from the journals.

This activity will help your team reflect on their best practices so they can identify what works and improve on what doesn't. I suggest keeping a workday journal for three to four weeks.

Activity 2:
The HP6 Assessment

Overview: High performers typically measure well in six high-performance habits: seeking clarity, generating energy, raising necessity, increasing productivity, developing influence, and demonstrating courage.

Objective: To see how you score in the HP6 and determine ways to improve.

Preparation: No prep is needed for this activity.

Materials: No materials are needed for this activity.

Step 1: Have each member of your team take the HP6 Assessment.[46] You should take it, too.

Step 2: Collectively discuss your results.

Step 3: Ask each of your staff to come up with a plan for improvement.

We all have improvements to make—the problem is, most of us don't know how to identify them. The HP6 Assessment is a fantastic tool to help us identify our weaknesses so we can improve them.

---

46   "What's Your Success Score? Get 6 Scores that Predict Your Long-Term Success Potential," The Burchard Group, accessed November 13, 2020, https://brendon.mykajabi.com/hp6-assessment.

CHAPTER 10

GROWTH AND CONTRIBUTION

*You have brilliance in you, your contribution is valuable, and the
art you create is precious. Only you can do, and you must.*

—SETH GODIN

One of my friends is tremendously competitive. A lot of my
friends are, but this guy takes it to the extreme. I'm competitive,
too, so when he challenged me to a triathlon, I quickly accepted.

A triathlon consists of three different sports, one right after the
other. The race disciplines are swimming, biking, and running.
Triathlons take place all over the world. (There are some varia-
tions that include different sports, but these three are the most
common.)

I accepted the challenge, even though I barely knew how to
swim. No kidding. At the time, I could barely swim the length
of a backyard swimming pool. I did what people call Tarzan
swimming—swimming with my head out of the water the entire
time and splashing—a lot. I also didn't own a bike and could run
for only short distances. I was a weight-lifting, strength guy—
endurance wasn't my thing.

I accepted the challenge anyway. I'm competitive, and I really wanted to beat my friend at his own game.

The race was less than a month away, and I was completely freaked out. I was out of shape and had no idea what to use or what to wear. What was I going to do?

To help prepare, someone suggested I read *Total Immersion* by Terry Laughlin. (It's a book that teaches you how to master the art of swimming. It's kind of like the Bible for swimming.) So I did, from cover to cover, and got in the pool every day until I learned how to swim. I borrowed a bike from a friend and researched the other equipment I would need for the cycling component, and I researched what I would need to run in the triathlon, too, as well as what I should eat and drink along the journey.

Finally, the day of the race arrived, and you know what? I *beat* my friend. My feet were a bloody mess—because I thought it would save time to run without putting on socks—but I didn't care. To me, it was worth it because I set a challenging goal and accomplished it. I learned new skills, worked continuously to improve them, and grew, both as an athlete and as a person.

And all of the sudden, I had a purpose. I was no longer just working out to "look good"; I was training for something specific—a race on the calendar, at a cool location, with friends and family. Before long, I was training for and competing in a half Ironman. Not too long after that, I was finishing the full-length Ironman version of the race in Louisville, Kentucky. The mental fortitude needed to complete an Ironman triathlon is just as critical as physical endurance. During the process, my mind grew, too.

If my friend hadn't challenged me to a triathlon, my life would be drastically different. I wouldn't have met other triathletes or adopted the Ironman mindset—"Anything Is Possible." You never know when a single challenge or interaction will change the course of your life. Today, I compete in Ironman races regularly (at the time of this printing, I have over a hundred races under my belt, including twenty-two Ironman triathlons[47]), even though not too long ago, I barely knew how to swim.

What trips most people up with growth is purpose and knowing their why. If they don't, it's easier to give up when things get tough. This applies to learning the Secure Methodology and anything else in life, including cybersecurity.

AI IS COMING FOR US

In the Secure Methodology, growth and improvement comes from practicing the seventh step, kaizen. To compete in my first triathlon, I had to embrace uncertainty and discomfort. I had no idea if I would be able to beat my friend or if I could even finish the race, and the training was tough. (I also fell at least a dozen times before I learned how to unclip from my bike pedals.) Even though I had bloody feet, I did finish and I beat my friend. I made a commitment to continuous improvement, so I worked hard and figured it out. I grew.

I also knew my why, which drove necessity. Necessity, as they often say, is the mother of all invention.

We are losing the cybersecurity war because our technical employees lack the people and leadership skills needed to communicate effectively. Leadership isn't just about leading others;

---

47   "Christian Espinosa (Ironracer)," Athlinks, accessed November 13, 2020, https://www.athlinks.com/athletes/300420786.

it's also about leading yourself through difficult and uncertain times, where the rubber meets the road.

Our technical team also often lacks the inner confidence to innovate outside the status quo. The Secure Methodology is a step-by-step process to help get them develop those people skills, but true growth and development won't happen unless we embrace kaizen and work to constantly improve.

And time is of the essence because every day, AI is getting better and better. We hear about it all the time. More factories and business are automating their processes and replacing human beings with machines. Amazon has a store in Seattle with no human cashiers—all goods are sold through Just Walk Out Technology, a system that can detect when items are taken off the shelf (or put back) and track them in a virtual cart. When the shopper is done, they can leave the store, and Amazon will charge them (via their preferred payment method) for the items they carried out with them. No human contact is required.[48]

It's surreal, but expect to see more of this in the not-so-distant future. Processes that are either technical or don't require human interaction (or both) will slowly but surely become automated. Machines are more efficient and cost effective than humans, not to mention safer. A machine won't have an accident on the conveyor belt or *cause* an accident on the DC Beltway, unless of course, the machines or driverless cars are hacked. Machines won't get tired after twelve hours of surgery and *will* be able to review medical imaging more granularly in order to detect cancers and other diseases.

---

48 "Just Walk Out: Technology by Amazon," Amazon, accessed June 3, 2020, https://justwalkout.com/.

Machines and computers will automate away a lot of jobs humans have today. It's only a matter of time. The window of time for surviving (not thriving) in life with limited people skills is quickly shrinking.

THE IMPACT ON CYBERSECURITY

AI already impacts cybersecurity to a degree. For example, there are many different software programs to assist with penetration testing and malware defenses, all powered by AI. Technology is making this aspect of cybersecurity easier and less human dependent—the gap between man and machine is tightening every day.

At some point, the gap is going to close completely, and technology will surpass humans. We used to calculate math by hand; now most of us are completely dependent on a calculator. Spreadsheets are the same way. Can you imagine doing business without them? Well, we used to. Right now, many of us live our lives independent of AI (for the most part), but eventually, that will change.

In cybersecurity, technology is only going to get better, and if you're a technical person, there's a good chance a machine and automation is coming for your job. That's why developing your people skills is critical, now more than ever. Machines can't replace jobs that require compassion, expressions of gratitude, and other qualities that make us human. AI is going to take over technical and process-oriented jobs, but human-facing jobs will remain because a machine can't replace the human soul, at least not yet. People skills are going to be even more valuable tomorrow than they are today.

GROWTH

You want your technical team to improve their people skills so they can grow and contribute to the cybersecurity industry and help win the war. If your technical team embraces the concepts in this book, their people skills will improve. Your *smartest people in the room* (in IQ only) will be able to communicate more effectively (both internally and externally) and work well with others to solve problems. It's also less likely they will be replaced by a machine.

When the people skills of your technical team improve, protecting your sensitive data and devices (and winning the cyberwar) becomes much easier. Growth and contribution become easier, too.

When your team practices kaizen, step 7 in the Secure Methodology, they start to see real growth. Because they better understand that everyone sees the world differently, they alter their communication and the way they interact with others. They start to transform their behavior in order to improve.

Many technical people don't like going to work because they don't like interacting with the people on their team. If they had it their way, they'd work alone.

---

49   2045 Strategic Social Initiative (website), http://2045.com/.

It's unrealistic to think that's a genuine possibility. Everyone has to work with *someone*, and if they don't, there's a very good chance their job will go to a machine soon anyway. No one can work alone indefinitely. Eventually, everyone has to deal with *someone* they don't like. Even if you're an independent contractor, you will have to deal with prospects and clients.

This isn't a problem siloed to the cybersecurity industry—we all have to deal with a bad apple every now and then. That's why I designed the skills in the Secure Methodology to provide *everyone* with the tools they need to deal with dissension, arguments, or a difference of opinion. Each step helps improve communication for everyone so we can all work together more harmoniously (even with the people we don't like). When we do, growth happens.

MY 6-INCH SCAR

The last football game of my senior high school year was a state playoff game, and I tore three of the four ligaments in my knee. I had to have surgery—a screw was put in my knee to reattach my MCL to my knee, causing a 6-inch scar on my inner knee. I was in a cast for nearly four months and lost my Air Force Academy qualification.

In order to regain my acceptance, I had to rehabilitate my knee and get it back to normal. I had to prove I was physically fit and in good enough condition to qualify. So I worked every day until my knee was fully healed and I was once again accepted into the Air Force Academy. In order to regain my qualification, I had to practice kaizen.

CONTRIBUTION

Growth isn't the last stop on our journey—it's *contribution*. Once we get our technical team to grow, how do we then get them to *contribute*?

Contribution helps us feel fulfilled, and it's the responsibility of everyone to give back. We should all share with the world or our circles of influence what we've learned so we can not only work together to stop cyberattacks but help improve the lives of others around us as well.

I have found that contribution comes naturally. In order to communicate effectively and work together to solve problems, our technical team needs to grow. Once they do, contribution comes in the form of more cybersecurity wins. By defeating the bad guys and protecting company data and devices from cybercriminals, your technical employees contribute to the organization and the cybersecurity industry. As you grow and see success, your need to contribute should increase. Your need to go from student to teacher, from dabbler to master, should emerge.

Technical leadership helps fight cybercrime, too, but they contribute in a different way. If they follow the Secure Methodology, they will evolve their point of view and be comfortable hiring and working with people who are smarter than them. They will grow to a point where they no longer care about being the smartest person in the room. They will also understand that everyone has a different and unique skillset that when combined, will contribute to the success of their organization and the cybersecurity industry. Technical leaders who embrace these skills can help *others* grow and contribute. That's their contribution.

CONTRIBUTE TO SOMETHING
GREATER THAN YOURSELF

Where would we as a society be if no one contributed?

Contribution in cybersecurity is important, too, both for you as the leader of an organization with data to protect and for your technical team. If you're looking for ways to increase your technical team's contribution to the world of cybersecurity, the Open Web Application Security Project® (OWASP)[50] is a great place to start.

I'm a huge fan of OWASP. It's a good example of what can happen when brilliant people collaborate and contribute to something greater than themselves.

FULFILLMENT

The Secure Methodology offers a side benefit. Circling back to the six human needs, growth and contribution are the needs of the spirit and lead to fulfillment.

Many people think achieving financial or professional success will make them happy and fulfilled, but I have found that isn't the case. If you're unfulfilled, you can have a full bank account and reach a career pinnacle, but you will always feel as if something is missing.

If you're unfulfilled, material possessions only mask fundamental unhappiness. If you're unhappy and you make $50,000 a year, you're still going to be unhappy if you make $500,000 a year. An increase in salary doesn't instantly make you happier—

---

50 Open Web Application Security Project (website), https://owasp.org/.

if you're unhappy, more money usually amplifies it because you discover the money doesn't bring fulfillment. What's stopping you from being fulfilled and happy now?

Growth and contribution (for both the technical team and technical leadership) lead to personal fulfillment. Most of us get fulfillment from contributing to something bigger or greater than ourselves because progress is what makes people feel happy. When there is a lack of progress, we feel stagnant, unfulfilled, and in some cases, depressed. The point of life is to feel fulfilled; that's why growth and contribution are the ultimate goals of the Secure Methodology.

EMPOWERMENT

We want people who are empowered. Empowered people make things better because they feel their contributions are noticed. They are acknowledged and feel like part of the team. They make our industry better, and they better equip us to win the cybersecurity war. Empowered people are more likely to win the internal war, too, and it's our responsibility as leaders to empower our people.

Growth and contribution empower your technical team to do something for themselves—they aren't solely working to make the company better. Improved communication and the ability to work with others successfully to solve problems are skills they can take with them anywhere. Enhanced people skills are helpful in every work and social situation.

The tactics in this book can be applied to everyday life, not just cybersecurity. When communication improves at work, it improves in our personal lives as well because being aware of differences and acknowledging challenges in the workplace translates at home, too. If you can monotask at work, you can probably get more done outside of work as well. The Secure Methodology can help improve all aspects of life.

Along the journey, if you're a technical employee, you may discover you don't like cybersecurity. You may discover you're passionate about something else instead. *Good for you.* Go after your dreams and leave the success trap.

DID YOU GIVE UP ON YOUR DREAMS?

Have you seen the movie *Up in the Air*? It stars George Clooney who portrays a guy who is hired to fire people.

In the movie, Clooney says one thing to someone he's about to fire that really sticks out:

"How much did they first pay you to give up on your dreams?"

This happens in real life all the time. People work at jobs they hate and aren't aligned with for perceived comfort and stability. Paper tigers take this path—they want the money but don't care about the industry. We want people who care about cybersecurity, about making a difference, and who care to contribute.

Do you think the employee Clooney fired contributed much?

Contribution requires passion, and this is where courage, one of those six high-performance habits, comes into play. It takes courage to follow what you are passionate about and what turns you on. Imagine how many more contributions there would be to our society if people did what they felt drawn to do, rather than what they feel has been defined as "safe, stable, and responsible."

By following the steps in the Secure Methodology, people learn themselves better. If cybersecurity is not for them, they should leave. Employers should hire the eager and passionate people desiring to grow and contribute.

Most people spend their entire lives doing something they hate. They tell themselves every day that they're going to make a change and do something they love, but they don't. Instead, they sit and complain about it for the rest of their lives.

If you've discovered your passion along this journey, congratulations. The Secure Methodology is a journey of self-discovery, and like I've hammered on about throughout this chapter, the skills outlined within are skills you can take anywhere. They are meant to help you improve your *people and life* skills and can be applied to every industry.

When I agreed to compete in my first triathlon, I had a month to train. I didn't know how to swim, I didn't own a bike, and could run less than one mile. I was completely out of my league, but I didn't care. I had it in my mind that I was going to compete and "figure it out."

I practiced every day and grew stronger, both mentally and physically. I trained, did my research, and prepared. When the day of the race came, I nailed it and beat my super-smack-talking buddy at his own game. (If there was an award for smack-talking, he'd for sure win that competition.) It was a great day, and now I compete regularly in triathlons and Ironman competitions.

I want the same for cybersecurity. I want my technical colleagues to follow the Secure Methodology and improve their people skills so they can grow and contribute to the industry in a more meaningful way. I want the industry to improve so we can do a better job overall of protecting our data and devices from cybercriminals. I also want meaningful contribution to the industry because it will lead to fulfillment. I want us all to lead a fulfilled, meaningful life, and growth and contribution will help get us there.

CONCLUSION

In basketball, everyone wants to slam dunk in a game because they think it's cool, but it's a difficult move, especially if you're still learning the game. First, you have to learn how to dribble, and then you have to learn how to shoot. From there, you have to learn how to do a layup, and then, if you have the skills and can jump high enough, you can learn how to dunk. Then, and only then, can you learn how to *slam* dunk. It should be the last thing you learn in basketball. Fundamentals come first.

In cybersecurity, we're trying to teach everyone how to slam dunk without teaching them anything about the game of basketball. We're skipping over all the fundamentals because we've overcomplicated the industry. We've made our solutions and processes complex, when we should make them simple.

Most tend to gravitate toward the status quo in cybersecurity. Thinking back to *The Matrix* reference earlier, many technical people take the blue pill. They're comfortable with what they're doing (posturing, bullying, and talking over other people's heads) and what they're offering (complicated frameworks, compliance checklists, next-gen products, etc.). They don't want to know the truth: people skills and simple risk-based solutions would move the industry closer to winning the war than posturing and complexity.

If something isn't working, it should be changed, but because these technical people communicate poorly, the conversations rarely change. People are stuck even though things aren't working.

We should examine our behavior, and if the results your behavior produces do not align with your goals, you should change. This is how perpetual growth and meaningful contribution happen in any industry.

For the cybersecurity industry specifically, we want our technical employees to examine their people skills and change them (if necessary) to align with their goals and objectives as well as their organization's mission. The goal is for our technical team and leaders to grow and contribute to the cybersecurity industry in a more meaningful way, and the best way to accomplish this is through enhanced people skills and the Secure Methodology.

THE SECURE METHODOLOGY

The Secure Methodology is a journey, and it isn't the same for everyone because all are tied to a different set of rules—we each have a different territory map. No matter what our map reads, however, there's something we all can learn, because even the most people-savvy of us have people and life skills with room to grow.

The Secure Methodology steps with kaizen in the middle.

Each step in the methodology leads to a more meaningful contribution in the cybersecurity industry. To briefly recap:

In *Step 1: Awareness*, we talked about blind spots and how putting ourselves in the shoes of others will broaden our perspectives. We discussed the difference between uninformed optimism and informed realism and that awareness means preferring the latter.

The subject of *Step 2: Mindset* was mindset, and without the right one, we aren't amenable to change. We also aren't motivated to make a *commitment* to change. To succeed in cybersecurity and win the war, we need to take the red pill, not the blue one, and embrace growth and change.

Step 3: Acknowledgment teaches that without recognition, technical employees become disengaged and focused on the wrong thing. We also talked about the "sandwich approach" and how to build rapport quickly using acknowledgment.

Step 4: Communication followed to balance the other six steps, the center support of the seesaw. First, we familiarized ourselves with the negative impact of "geek speak," "robot talk," and poor listening skills, and then we covered the difference between left- and right-brained people and how to alter communication to be more effective.

Next, *Step 5: Monotasking* explained about how multitasking makes you a slave to everyone else's time. We learned that multitasking can lead to anxiety and a lack of presence and quality and that to reclaim your agenda, you need to monotask and schedule block time.

In *Step 6: Empathy*, the focus was on the human connection and mankind's inherent—albeit misguided—need to focus on differences. We talked about two different categories of empathy (cognitive and affective) and ended with the goal to find and emphasize similarities.

Finally, in *Step 7: Kaizen*, we highlighted the need for constant and never-ending improvement. We discovered there are two types of people in the world, masters and dabblers, and that true mastery takes time. We learned to embrace uncertainty and take baby steps.

The Secure Methodology is a surefire way to kick-start your technical team's people skills and get them to communicate effectively, work together to solve problems, and contribute to the industry in a meaningful, substantial way. That's how we're going to win the cybersecurity war and our own internal war, too.

A FEW SMALL REQUESTS

Now that you're done reading *The Smartest Person in the Room*, I have a few small requests.

If you're a corporate leader, I want you to acknowledge your technical staff, how hard they've worked to get where they are, and how the odds in cybersecurity are stacked against them. If you've learned something, I want you to share this book with others, and if you have questions, I want you to contact me.

If you're a technical leader, I want you to lead with your heart. I want you to realize there are different perspectives and that we all are connected on a *human* level. I want you to stop posturing, bullying, and talking over other people's heads, and I want you to stop hiring paper tigers. I want you to be open to change.

And if you're a technical employee, I want you to be open to change, too. I want you to change your paradigm and unbind your current way of thinking. I want you to make decisions based on your total intelligence (heart, body, and mind), and I want you to monotask.

It is my sincere hope that whoever reads this book learns something and finds meaning and fulfillment because of it. The Secure Methodology was designed with technical people and leaders in mind, but the steps outlined inside can benefit everyone. This book isn't restricted to technical fields.

Some people go through their entire lives and want a different career, a different relationship, a different *anything* but never change their behavior. Cybersecurity is the same. We're getting killed out there, but no one changes a thing. No wonder we're losing the war.

It's time to start winning. With enhanced people skills and the Secure Methodology, our technical team can learn to communicate more constructively, work together more harmoniously, and contribute to the cybersecurity industry in a more meaningful and successful way.

I know I've blurred the lines in this book between personal development and cybersecurity—that was intentional. I've always been a believer that if you want the world to get better, you have to get better. Your inner world must improve before the outer world will improve. My intent with this book was to produce something full of life hacks with an *infinite* shelf life, rather than another book full of technical tricks with a *finite* shelf life.

WHAT NOW?

Visit my website (www.christianespinosa.com) or contact me at info@christianespinosa.com for group and individual training and coaching on the Secure Methodology, or to book me as a speaker. You can also contact my company, www.alpinesecurity.com, for all your cybersecurity needs.

ACKNOWLEDGMENTS

I used to think I could do it all by myself—that I didn't need anyone. That it was me against the world. Along the way, I realized I need people and support and that how I show up in each moment counts. I'm grateful for my journey in life and especially for those who have impacted me. I want to thank:

- Jennifer and Alice—for unconditionally loving, believing in, and supporting me
- Coach Kelly—for peeling back the layers, asking the tough questions, and revealing my blind spots and incongruence
- Carla—for your insightful perspective, love, and COVID-19 journey
- Lisa—for diligently working with me to make this book a reality
- Everyone mentioned in this book (names, dates, and places have been changed, but you'll know who you are) who provided insight and inspiration
- My former employers who provided great examples of what to do and what not to do
- Past and current employees of Alpine Security
- The Iron Hombres

- My fellow HPM and Genius Network cohorts for showing me what is possible, how to be better, and that I'm not alone (or crazy)
- Freelance and Alpine Security clients
- Everyone in personal development who has influenced me
- Everyone who said something nice to me or showed appreciation, especially the cashier at Schnucks in Fairview Heights, Illinois, that day
- Nightwish
- All of the smartest people in the room
- Everyone who picked up a copy of this book who desires to be better and effect positive change

ABOUT THE AUTHOR

CHRISTIAN ESPINOSA is the Founder and CEO of Alpine Security, a cybersecurity engineer, certified high-performance coach, professor, and lover of heavy metal music and spicy food. He's also an Air Force veteran and Ironman triathlete. He used to value being the smartest guy in the room, only to realize that his greatest contribution to the fight against cybercrime is his ability to bring awareness to the issue through effective communication. Christian is a speaker, coach, and trainer in the Secure Methodology, helping to make the smartest people in the room the best leaders in the field. For more information, visit www.christianespinosa.com.

Printed in Great Britain
by Amazon